THE REVELS PLAYS

Founder Editor
Clifford Leech 1958–71

General Editors
F. David Hoeniger, E. A. J. Honigmann and J. R. Mulryne

THE OLD WIVES TALE

Wandering knight and dragon, from *Valentine and Orson: the two sons of the Emperor of Greece*. Printed by J. R. for T. Passinger. London, 1688. By courtesy of the Osborne Collection of Early Children's Books, Toronto Public Library.

THE REVELS PLAYS

THE
OLD WIVES
TALE

GEORGE PEELE

Edited by
Patricia Binnie

MANCHESTER
UNIVERSITY PRESS

THE JOHNS HOPKINS
UNIVERSITY PRESS

© Patricia Binnie 1980

First published 1980
by Manchester University Press
Oxford Road, Manchester M13 9PL
ISBN 0 7190 1525 1

Published in the United States of America, 1980, by
The Johns Hopkins University Press
Baltimore, Maryland 21218
ISBN 0–8018–2410–9

Library of Congress Catalogue Card Number 79–48011

British Library Cataloguing in Publication Data

Peele, George.
    The old wives tale. – (The revels plays).
    I. Title. II. Binnie, Patricia.
    III. Series.
    822'.3   PR2734.04
    UK ISBN 0–7190–1525–1
    US ISBN 0–8018–2410–9

Printed and bound in Great Britain
by W & J Mackay Limited, Chatham

Contents

General Editors' Preface

The series known as the Revels Plays was conceived by Clifford Leech. The idea for the series emerged in his mind, as he explained in his preface to the first of the Revels Plays in 1958, from the success of the New Arden Shakespeare. The aim of the new group of texts was 'to apply to Shakespeare's predecessors, contemporaries and successors the methods that are now used in Shakespeare editing'. The plays chosen were to include well known works from the early Tudor period to about 1700, as well as others less familiar but of literary and theatrical merit: 'the plays included,' Leech wrote, 'should be such as to deserve and indeed demand performance.' We owe it to Clifford Leech that the idea became reality. He set the high standards of the series, ensuring that editors of individual volumes produced work of lasting merit, equally useful for teachers and students, theatre directors and actors. Clifford Leech remained General Editor until 1971, supervising the first seventeen volumes to be published.

The Revels Plays are now under the direction of three General Editors, F. David Hoeniger, E. A. J. Honigmann and J. R. Mulryne. The publishers, originally Methuen, are now Manchester University Press, with Johns Hopkins University Press as co-publisher. Yet, despite these changes, the format and essential character of the series will continue, and it is hoped that its editorial standards will be maintained. Except for some work in progress, the General Editors intend, in expanding the series, to concentrate for the immediate future on plays from the period 1558–1642, and may include a small number of non-dramatic works of interest to students of drama. Some slight changes have been forced by considerations of cost. For example, in editions from 1978, notes to the Introduction are placed

vi

together at the end, not at the foot of the page. Collation and commentary notes will continue, however, to appear on the relevant pages.

The text of each Revels play, in accordance with established practice in the series, is edited afresh from the original text of best authority (in a few instances, texts), but spelling and punctuation are modernised and speech headings are silently made consistent. Elisions in the original are also silently regularised, except where metre would be affected by the change; since 1968 the '-ed' form is used for non-syllabic terminations in past tenses and past participles ('-'d' earlier), and '-èd' for syllabic ('-ed' earlier). The editor emends, as distinct from modernises, his original only in instances where error is patent, or at least very probable, and correction persuasive. Act divisions are given only if they appear in the original or if the structure of the play clearly points to them. Those act and scene divisions not found in the original are provided unobtrusively in small type and in square brackets. Square brackets are also used for any other additions to or changes in the stage directions of the original.

Revels Plays do not provide a variorum collation, but only those variants which require the critical attention of serious textual students. All departures of substance from 'copy-text' are listed, including any relineation and those changes in punctuation which involve to any degree a decision between alternative interpretations; but not such accidentals as turned letters, nor necessarily additions to stage directions whose editorial nature is already made clear by the use of brackets. Press corrections in the 'copy-texts' are likewise included. Of later emendations of the text, only those are given which as alternative readings still deserve attention.

One of the hallmarks of the Revels Plays is the thoroughness of their annotations. Besides explaining the meaning of difficult words and passages, the editor provides comments on customs or usage, text or stage-business—indeed, on anything he judges pertinent and helpful. Each volume contains a Glossarial Index to the Commentary, in which particular attention is drawn to meanings for words not listed in *O.E.D.*

The Introduction to a Revels play assesses the authority of the 'copy-text' on which it is based, and discusses the editorial methods employed in dealing with it; the editor also considers his play's date and (where relevant) sources, together with its place in the work of the author and in the theatre of its time. Stage history is offered, and in the case of a play by an author not previously represented in the series a brief biography is given.

It is our hope that plays edited in this fashion will promote further scholarly and theatrical investigation of one of the richest periods in theatrical history.

F. DAVID HOENIGER

E. A. J. HONIGMANN

J. R. MULRYNE

Acknowledgments

I began work on *The Old Wives Tale* under the general editorship of the late Clifford Leech and completed it under the direction of one of the present general editors, David Hoeniger. I can never adequately express my gratitude to my two colleagues for their encouragement and patience, and for their rich insights into the play, which helped give form to my own views. From the time the task of general editor passed to David Hoeniger, he has given me help when I became puzzled by textual and interpretative tangles. Especially as this edition neared completion, he gave of his time without stint, and I am convinced that the work would not have been finished without his aid.

I should also like to thank the librarians at the Pforzheimer, London, Folger, and Bryn Mawr Libraries. Their assistance made it possible for me to accomplish my research.

I am indebted to the Canada Council for granting me a leave fellowship, 1972–73, to pursue my work in England.

To those producers of *The Old Wives Tale*—David Blostein, Derek Forbes, Richard Proudfoot, and G. B. Shand—who painstakingly reconstructed, on paper and in conversations, their methods of productions—I wish to give great thanks. Editing Peele's play has been a delight, but they have 'chosen the better part'.

In the years that have passed since I began this edition, I have become myself an old wife, and my husband Andrew and my son James are to be thanked for helping me to tell the tale.

P.B.

Abbreviations

Apuleius   *The Golden Ass*, trans. W. Aldington, 1566. Loeb
           Library, 1915.
Cheffaud   P. H. Cheffaud, *George Peele (1558–1596?)*. Paris,
           1913.
Dekker   *The Dramatic Works of Thomas Dekker*, ed. Fredson
           Bowers. 4 vols. Cambridge, 1953–61.
Horne   David Horne, *The Life and Minor Works of George
           Peele*. New Haven, 1952. (Yale Peele, vol. I).
Jonson   *Ben Jonson*, ed. C. H. Herford and P. and E. Simp-
           son. 11 vols. Oxford, 1925–52.
Nashe   *The Works of Thomas Nashe*, ed. R. B. McKerrow,
           revised by F. P. Wilson. 5 vols. Oxford, 1958.
Tilley   Morris P. Tilley, *A Dictionary of the Proverbs in Eng-
           land in the Sixteenth and Seventeenth Centuries*. Ann
           Arbor, 1950.

EDITIONS OF THE OLD WIVES TALE

A. The quarto of 1595 (= Q)
    QB   British Library Quarto.
    QD   Dyce Quarto (Victoria and Albert Museum).
    QH   Huntington Library Quarto.
    QP   Pforzheimer Library Quarto.

B. Modern editions
    Baskervill   *Elizabethan and Stuart Plays*, ed. C. R. Bas-
                 kervill, V. B. Heltzer, and A. H. Nethercot,
                 1934.
    Blair   Robert L. Blair, unpublished dissertation,
                 University of Illinois, 1936.

Bullen *The Works of George Peele*, ed. A. H. Bullen, 1888, vol. I.

Dyce 1828 *The Works of George Peele*, ed. Alexander Dyce, 1828, vol. I.

Dyce 1861 Revised edition of *OWT*, in *The Dramatic and Poetical Works of Robert Greene and George Peele*, ed. Alexander Dyce, 1861.

Dyce Reading is common to both editions.

Gummere *Representative English Comedies*, ed. F. B. Gummere (General Editor C. M. Gayley), 1903, vol. I.

Hook *The Life and Works of George Peele*, ed. F. S. Hook, 1970, vol III. (Yale Peele)

McIlwraith *Five Elizabethan Comedies*, ed. A. K. McIlwraith, 1934.

All quotations from *The Old Wives Tale* are from the Revels edition or the British Library quarto. All other Peele quotations are from the Yale edition.

Shakespearean quotations are from *The Complete Works of William Shakespeare*, ed. Peter Alexander, London, 1951.

Introduction

George Peele was born in London c. 25 July 1556, and after several years of privation and illness, died on 9 November 1596. If *The Old Wives Tale* was written c. 1593[1], it dates from the last years of Peele's life and may be a high point in his art, rather than the mangled fragment it has sometimes been considered. In *The Old Wives Tale* he skilfully (with a light but sure touch) integrates characteristics of his other works: proficiency in lyric (as shown in passages in all the plays and poems), reliance on visual spectacle for dramatic effect (as in the various shows and entertainments), and an affinity for pastoral and romance (seen perhaps most strongly in *The Arraignment of Paris*). *The Old Wives Tale*, while being lyrical, spectacular, and romantic, at the same time encourages its audience to distance itself from complete identification with and involvement in these aspects, and to enter the world of Madge's old tale sympathetically, but also from a perspective of wit and intellectual understanding. As the chief aim of this introduction will be to look at the unique way Peele handles the conventions of romantic tale-telling, tempering 'fantasy' with 'rationality', one should note the connections Peele maintained, throughout his life, with the world of wit.[2]

Peele's background was intellectual. He received his first education at Christ's Hospital, where his father, James Peele, was Clerk, an office which entailed keeping the school's books, as well as teaching. In addition to these duties, his father wrote city pageants, and knowing this one can imagine how early were the origins of Peele's sympathy for the form. When Peele left London for Christ Church, Oxford, he entered a college noted for the strength of its dramatic tradition.[3] He received his B.A. in June 1577, and his M.A. in July 1579, and, as Frank Hook

I

notes in his introduction to *Edward I*, Peele remained proud of his achievements as a scholar:

> a curious *explicit* at the end of the play (sig. L3v) reads: '*Yours*. By *George Peele Maister of | Artes in Oxenford*'. Peele was evidently sufficiently proud of his Oxford degree to make it part of a characteristic subscription to his compositions.[4]

While Peele was at Oxford, his friend William Gager wrote a poem praising him for his particular talent—mixing serious remarks and clever jests: '*Oxoniae fateor subitu[m] mirabar acumen, | Et tua cu[m] lepidis seria mista iocis.*'[5] This reputation remained with Peele throughout his life. The joke book *The Merry Conceited Jests of George Peele* (1607) is certainly far from factual biography, but it probably derived from things basically true about Peele's personality—high spirits, cleverness, and wit. After leaving Oxford, Peele maintained connections with his university friends, now living near the Inns of Court in Holborn.[6] His association with young intellectuals of his time may possibly have involved him in the Harvey/Nashe quarrel.[7] The court play *The Arraignment of Paris*, and pageants written for court and city, are evidence of Peele's attraction to sophisticated, witty, artistically self-aware genres.

In *The Old Wives Tale* one encounters the union of the characteristics Gager noted in Peele—the serious and the jesting. It is the tension between the two that leads one to say of *The Old Wives Tale* (as Robert Greene said of Peele himself) that it is 'in some things rarer, in nothing inferior.'[8]

It may be a legacy from the jesting spirit of George Peele that such a brief, graceful, lighthearted 'toy' of a play presents so many tough problems, textual and critical. Was it Peele, in fact, who wrote *The Old Wives Tale*? Could it have been intended for a special occasion? What kind of manuscript lies behind the quarto printing? Is the quarto a truncated version of a longer original?[9] And, most difficult, what dramatic and emotional effects does Peele intend? Are the romantic episodes in the play to be taken seriously, or is romance mocked throughout? Is Peele in control of his material, or does it run away with him? Is the play, as Northrop Frye suggested, 'one of the loveliest in the language'[10], or is Hazleton Spencer justified in omitting it from his anthology of Elizabethan plays 'without much regret . . . Most of it is sad stuff'?[11] These questions will govern the shape of this discussion, but in offering answers to them, one should take the Head's advice to the two sisters, 'Gently dip, but not too deep' (664); for most of the matters cannot be solved conclusively.

AUTHORSHIP AND DATE

The 1595 quarto of *The Old Wives Tale* has on its title page 'Written by G.P.'. That G.P. is George Peele is impossible to prove, but there are sufficient reasons for believing the work to be his. Isaac Reed, in *Biographica Dramatica* (1782),[12] was, as Hook notes, 'the first to ascribe this play to Peele in print' and it has been so ascribed from that time.[13] The fact that works by Peele, and those attributed to him, do not possess an outstandingly distinctive style, together with the fact that each work is of a different kind from each of the others,[14] makes certainty about the authorship of *The Old Wives Tale* difficult; but some arguments seem plausible.

Hook presents as internal evidence of Peele's authorship the presence of verbal parallels between *The Old Wives Tale* and other works ('the phrase "the chalkie Cliffs of Albion" (*O.W.T.*, line 136), a favourite with Peele, also appears in the holograph of *Anglorum Feriae* (43) and with minor variations in line 3 of *A Farewell* and line 183 of *Polyhymnia*');[15] and also offers as evidence the frequent use of certain devices of verbal repetition.[16] One might compare:

> O Fortune cruel, cruel and unkind,
> Unkind in that we cannot find our sister,
> Our sister hapless in her cruel chance.   (141–3)

> Poore Colin thow arte going to the grounde:
> The love whom Thestilis hathe slaine,
> Harde harte, fair face fraught with disdaine:
> Disdaine in love a deadlie wounde.
> Wounde her swete love so deepe againe . . .
>   (*Arraignment*, 710–14)

To my mind, the resemblance between *The Old Wives Tale* and other works by Peele seems to be more one of mood than of concrete verbal parallels. I am aware that what I offer here as evidence is common to much early Elizabethan poetry (dramatic and non-dramatic); but, nevertheless, these characteristics do seem to be especially strong in Peele. With the device of repetition comes often a tone of deliberately crafted romantic poignancy (as in the first two of the following quotations) or of lusty exuberance (as in the last two):

> Hot sunne, coole fire, temperd with sweet aire,
> Black shade, fair nurse, shadow my white haire.
> Shine sun, burne fire, breathe aire, and ease mee,
> Black shade, fair nurse, shroud me and please me.
>
> (*David and Bethsabe*, 24–8)

> Wretched Eumenides, still unfortunate,
> Envied by Fortune, and forlorn by Fate   (*O.W.T.*, 718–19)

> what thing is love for (well I wot) love is a thing
> it is a pricke; it is a sting
> it is a prettie prettie thing   (*The Hunting of Cupid*, 12–14)

> Whenas the rye reach to the chin,
> And chopcherry, chopcherry ripe within . . .
> Then O, then O, then O my true love said,
> Till that time come again,
> She could not live a maid.   (*O.W.T.*, 78–9, 82–4)

As with these stylistic matters, the central dramatic contrivance of *The Old Wives Tale*—playing with the shifting relation of illusion to reality, of 'tale' to natural life, which includes a journey to the territory in which the two become indistinguishable—is a common one in Elizabethan drama; but Peele seems especially intrigued with the relationship. The characters in Madge's story enter to tell her tale for her; at the end of *The Arraignment of Paris*, Diana steps from the world of pastoral myth to present Queen Elizabeth, Queen of Second Troy, with the golden ball (1240.1); the Epilogue to *The Honour of the Garter* can affirm that his 'dreame' of past chivalric glories comes

true in the present moment with 'these newe advaunced Lords /
S. Georges Knights' (Epil., 6–7).

The date of *The Old Wives Tale* is likewise problematic. In 1594
the Queen's Men ('whether because they had ceased to be
modish, or because their finances had proved unable to stand
the strain of the plague years'[17]) had left London to perform in
the provinces, and the publication of the quarto of *The Old
Wives Tale* in 1595 was probably occasioned by the company's
financial difficulties (eight other plays were sold to publishers in
1594–95[18]). While this evidence suggests that the play was not
written later than 1594, a *terminus a quo* is less certain. The
'Leaving fair Po' speech (890–3) and the 'three blue beans . . .
rattle' phrase (686–7), being practically identical to passages in
Robert Greene's *Orlando Furioso*, indicate a close relation between the two plays; but the evidence seems to be that Peele
borrowed from Greene, rather than the other way round.[19] The
'Leaving fair Po' passage is more organic to the context of
Greene's play than it is to Peele's, and although the enchanter
Sacrapant (Sacripant in Greene) appears in both plays, 'Sacripante' is already in Ariosto's *Orlando*. It seems obvious that
Greene did not look to Peele's play to find a character present in
his immediate source. *Orlando* could not have been written
before mid-1588, as the allusion to the Spanish Armada
proves.[20] *The Old Wives Tale* was thus written between 1588 and
1594.

The one remaining clue which might help date the play, the
part Peele may have played in the Harvey/Nashe quarrel, also
proves a dead end. Though the character of Huanebango was
clearly conceived by Peele not merely as a parody of Gabriel
Harvey, some of Huanebango's lines (676, 683) contain elements of Harvey-mocking. Harvey's *Foure Letters* ridiculing
Greene were published in 1592; and Nashe's *Foure Letters Confuted*, his rejoinder to Harvey, appeared in 1593. Possibly, then,
if Peele were taking part in the quarrel, *The Old Wives Tale* was
written between 1592 and 1593. However, such a basis for
dating the play is inadequate; for in the verbal parodies which

are part of the characterisation of Huanebango, Peele was indulging in the common sport of making fun of the ragged hexameters of Richard Stanyhurst's *Aeneid* (1582) rather than specifically scoffing at Harvey's style.[21] In Huanebango we have a satiric portrait of *all* braggarts; he is kin to the Plautine *miles gloriosus* (270–71, 302–3, 306) and to the 'ruffler' and 'Bold Slasher' of folk drama.[22]

The precise date of the play is thus uncertain, but I would place it about 1593.

<h2 style="text-align:center">THE TEXT</h2>

All editions of the play have been based, directly or indirectly, on its first and only quarto, which appeared with the following title page:

> THE / Old Wiues Tale. / A pleasant conceited Come- / die, played by the Queenes Ma- / iesties players. / Written by G.P. / [Printer's large ornament] / Printed at London by *Iohn Danter*, and are to / be sold by *Raph Hancocke*, and *Iohn* / *Hardie*. 1595.

Hancock had been granted a licence to print the play on 16 April of the same year.[23] No manuscript has survived. For a play quarto of the time, this one is unusually short: approximately 1,200 lines long (970 in this edition). The text begins on A3 and ends on F3v. There are thus six gatherings, two of which are used only in part. The play's action is notable for its abrupt transitions from one strand of the plot to the next; for example, lines 252–67 (from Lampriscus to Madge to the Harvesters to Huanebango), and see also the many rapid shifts in the finale, lines 835 on. The Huanebango scenes present a problem, and one has reason to wonder whether Corebus and Booby were indeed meant to represent the same character. There are a few other irregularities in characters' names and speech headings: in the opening line, *Franticke* should be Frolic; the speech heading *Simon* at 479 should be *Churchwarden*; at 330 *Huau.* (properly *Huan.*) ought perhaps to be *Booby*;[24] and the earlier Celanta later (803.1–830) becomes Zelanto. On the other hand, misprints are rare, and the text itself seems lucid throughout, with hardly a patent error.

A. *The printing of the quarto: the proof-reader's corrections*[25]
The quarto of 1595, printed by John Danter, was evidently set up by competent workmen. In the previous year, Danter had printed Q1 of *Titus Andronicus*.[26] The printing is notably regular, with only minor variations in method. The collation is A1–F3v: A1, title page; A1v–A2v, blank; A3–F3v, text. The reason for the blank leaf A2 may be that the printer was not sure whether there might be a preface or address to the reader. Up to the end of signature E, there are regularly thirty lines of text (counting the catchword), but from then on the pages are one line shorter, perhaps deliberately for the sake of filling the final page, F3v, neatly.[27] The spacing of the stage directions varies little and is usually quite tight but neat, except for one instance where an Exit abbreviated to *ex.* is squeezed in, on sig. B2v, in such a way as to be almost lost sight of. Only on a few pages are the speech headings not quite perfectly aligned. While some of them are unabbreviated, a few are reduced excessively (*e.g.*, *Ol.* for Old Woman at the bottom of A4); but this appears to be due to two causes: the need at times to follow a long speech heading like *1. Brother* by a longer line of verse, and the desire to fit lines at the bottom of a page. There is, however, one variation: only on A3v and A4 are the speech headings always followed by a stop, elsewhere almost always by a colon, with only occasional exceptions. The compositors followed their copy well in the many transitions in the play from prose to verse or vice versa, and problems for an editor arise only because at some points the prose is quite metrical. A very few slips apart, the printing is reliable. The compositors appear to have followed a clear manuscript copy conscientiously and exactly, and to have had experience in setting up a play text.

The absence of any marked physical variation in the set up of pages suggests that if the printing of the play was shared among different workmen, their methods and degrees of competence were closely similar. On a basis of a thorough analysis of the spelling variants, Hook, the Yale editor, concluded that there were two compositors whose work was divided as follows: compositor A set up A3–B2v, C1–3, D3–E2v, and F3–F3v; compositor B set up B3–B4v, C3v–D2v, and E3–F2v.[28] But Hook admitted that the evidence is limited and the division he arrived at therefore tentative. Of the spelling variants he used, only the following are consistent between the two compositors, and in this short play of rambling action and many characters, they do not occur in sufficient quantity: Iack/Iacke, hir/her, doo/do, and goe/go; all other spellings he analysed are shared by the two compositors, even if one used one form far more frequently than the other. Yet except for slight modifications his argument is convincing. If the division is sound, it would indicate that the play was set up either *seriatim* or by half formes—the irregular speech headings with stop instead of colon on A3v and A4 point to the latter as a possibility. Further, such a division would suggest that, except at C3, one compositor took over the work from his companion always either at the end of a gathering or in the middle, after the fourth page. However, the irregularity at C3, implied in Hook's scheme, appears to be based only on the evidence of a single 'goe' spelling, and thus should be questioned. And for reasons already indicated, a third compositor appears to have been responsible for A3v and A4 alone. Examination of patterns of recurring damaged or unusual types proved inconclusive. Use of both roman and italic types is consistent throughout.

The running titles of the quarto are irregular in pattern. Most of the time, all three words, *Old Wiues Tale*, appear capitalised, but only on sheet D are they so throughout. On the other sheets, *Old Wiues tale* (small t) appears on B3, C, C2, E, E2, and F2; and *old Wiues tale* (small o and t) appears on A4v, B, C3, C4, E3, and E4. Moreover, of the latter, while the running title of C3 was reused at E3, and that of C4 at E4, those on A4v and B do not seem to fit. To conclude: clearly, it will be desirable for a scholar some time to subject all four extant copies of the quarto to a far more thorough bibliographical examination than has been possible for me. No hypothesis can here be advanced concerning the precise order of printing, and the suggested division among three compositors must be tentative. What can be asserted with conviction is that the physical appearance of the printed text in the quarto reveals no sign whatever to make one suspicious that the compositors did not follow conscientiously and completely their manuscript copy. On the whole, their work can be trusted.

There are but four extant copies of the 1595 quarto, and two of these are in a corrected state. The corrections occur, however, only in the inner forme of signature E. The Pforzheimer Library and Dyce copies are uncorrected; the British Library and Huntington Library copies preserve the corrections:

Dyce and Pforzheimer		*British Library and Huntington*
E 1v	rude (line 1)	rim
E2	Whose (15)	Who's
E4	goulden bird (9)	gouldē beard
	goulden bird (14)	gouldē beard
	tost (22)	iust
	quoiners . . . quine (22)	coiners . . . coine

The correction *rim* is appropriate, for *rude* appears clearly to be the typesetter's anticipation of *rude an incounter* (l. 3). The proof-reader likely checked the manuscript and restored the proper reading. *Whose* looks like a simple slip. There would have been no need for the proof-reader to check copy. The correction from *tost* to *iust*, however, has no justification, and one can only infer that the proof-reader arbitrarily made it.[29]

The corrected copies' *coiners . . . coine* looks like a modernisation of *quoiners . . . quine* (uncorrected copies). *O.E.D.*, under 'quoin', gives 'quine' as a variant spelling for 'coin'. As 'quine' is the more unusual spelling, it is probably what stood in the MS, it being unlikely that the compositor would substitute a more archaic spelling for a 'modern' one. The correction to *coiners . . . coine* may also reflect misunderstanding of Peele's meaning. 'To quine' (or 'quoine') meant to secure with a cornerstone, or keystone (quoin).[30] Could it be that the Clown is punning on getting money/setting up a household? 'God send us "coiners"; God send us housebuilders.' (In the state of matrimony one needs, as Zantippa knows, 'a house and a home' (637), as well as cash.) Here, therefore, again the proof-reader did not consult manuscript copy.

There remains the change, twice on E4, of *goulden bird* to *gouldē beard*, which represents an editorial crux. *golden birde* likewise appears on D4v (in all four copies), set up by the other compositor (A set up D4v; B set up E4). But it is difficult to see how *beard* could be misread as *bird*, and moreover by different compositors. As there is neither evidence nor likelihood that Peele himself checked any part of the text in the course of printing, we can again conclude that the proof-reader introduced the change for reasons other than the manuscript reading. For further discussion of the problem the reader is directed to the notes.[31]

Finally, the proof-reader missed a major variant in the inner forme of E (E3v and E4) from earlier in the play: Celanta (D4) becomes Zelanto (speech headings *Zelan.* or *Zela.*).[32] The variant provides further evidence for the casualness with which proof-reading occurred, as well as an example of the unfixed proper names in the play, a matter to which the discussion will now turn, but whose cause is probably to be found in the manuscript, not in the printing.

B. *The Booby/Corebus confusion, and the nature of the manuscript copy*

The most conspicuous example of unfixed names is that the Clown has two names. In the first Huanebango episode (264.1 ff.) the Braggart's servant is called Booby (both in the speech headings and in the text (l. 340)); in the second Huanebango episode (564.1 ff.) and in the scene with Celanta at the well (803.1 ff.) the servant is named Corebus. Between the first and second Huanebango episodes comes the incident in the churchyard (473.1 ff.) where Corebus first appears. On initial reading one assumes this character to be a different one from 'Booby'; then, in the second Huanebango scene, one finds that the characters are conflated. In what sort of MS could such a situation arise?

The Booby/Corebus crux seems at once to offer evidence that
Q. was not printed from prompt copy. An acting version of the
play would hardly contain such a character confusion. Additional evidence, which seems to eliminate the possibility of
prompt copy, is the nature of the stage directions. Their discur-
siveness is not characteristic of an acting version:

Enter the Two Brothers *in their shirts, with spades, digging.*
(613.1)

Enter [CELANTA] *the Foul Wench, to the well for water, with a pot in her*
hand.   (640.1–2)

Here they dig and descry the light under a little hill.   (629.1)[33]

She breaks her pitcher upon his head; then it thunders and lightens, and
HUANEBANGO *rises up.* HUANEBANGO *is deaf and cannot hear.*
(674.1–3)

Such stage directions rather convey how an author visualises the
action. The impression of leisureliness is further conveyed by
the descriptive tags which often accompany characters' proper
names:

Enter VENELIA *his lady, mad; and goes in again.*   (201.1)

Enter ZANTIPPA, *the Curst Daughter, to the well, with a pot in her hand.*
(636.1–2)

Concerning names of characters in the stage directions, in
prompt copy these tend to be consistent, whereas in *The Old*
Wives Tale what a character is called often changes, which could
indicate the author at work. Erestus, for instance, is first introduced:

Enter Senex at the cross, stooping to gather.   (143.1)

Later, 'Senex' is dropped, but the tone of the directions con-
tinues conversational, and Erestus' name is still unfixed:

Enter EUMENIDES *the Wandering Knight and the old man at the cross.*
(451.1 and 456.1)[34]

Enter VENELIA, *the Two Brothers, and he that was at the cross.*
(912.2–3)

It is in the dialogue that we find out the proper names of Madge, Clunch, Erestus, Calypha and Thelea; in the stage directions and speech headings they are 'Old Woman', 'Smith', 'Old man at the cross', and 'the Two Brothers'. Sacrapant is first intro-duced (351.1) by his proper name: '*Enter* SACRAPANT *in his study*', but is called 'the conjurer' at his next entrance (435.1). When he appears at 586.1 he is again called 'the conjurer', but 'Sacrapant' at his exit (610.1). Eumenides' first entrance (451.1) reads '*Enter* EUMENIDES *the Wandering Knight*'; later (499.1) his proper name only is used: 'EUMENIDES *awakes and comes to them*'; at 840.1–2 his proper name is omitted: '*Enter the Conjurer to the Wandering Knight*'.

A number of essential entries are omitted in the quarto, including those of Erestus at 315.1[35] and the Hostess at 787.1. At 586.1 it is necessary for the Furies to be on stage to carry off Huanebango, but their entrance is not marked. Also, after 473 adequate direction is not given for Eumenides. It is clear later that he has gone to sleep ('EUMENIDES awakes and comes to them', 499.1). The absence of these stage directions does not prove the theory that the underlying manuscript must have been the author's draft. Such evidence, taken by itself, merely shows that the manuscript can hardly have been prompt copy. But when it is considered in conjunction with the general nature of the stage directions and naming of the characters, then the case for the manuscript having been authorial indeed appears strong.[36] Another minor piece of evidence is the name 'Simon' given to the Churchwarden in the speech heading at 479. Simon may possibly preserve the name of the actor John Simonds (see 479n.), though we cannot be sure of this. At any rate, if the manuscript were prompt copy, the speech heading would likely have been changed to Churchwarden.

Before continuing with this argument, however, we need to attend to a different view, namely, that Q. was printed from a cut version of a longer play.[37] Harold Jenkins was the first to suggest that the text represents an abbreviated version of Peele's original intention, in his article 'Peele's *Old Wives Tale*'.[38] First, there is the brevity of the play; Jenkins finds it 'extremely, even unnaturally short' (p. 180). In addition, while agreeing that part of the dramatic method of *The Old Wives Tale* is akin to the method of folk tale, where actions are often unmotivated and transitions are sudden, he nevertheless thinks the action 'too huddled' and themes 'too slightly handled' (p. 178). Specific moments that give difficulty are:

1. Erestus' sudden question at 158 ('Was she fair?') has nothing to do with what the First Brother has just said, indicating cutting (p. 181).
2. Sacrapant's 'Hold thee there, friar!' (410) appears to be an interruption of a longer speech, now missing in the abridged version (p. 178).
3. We should see more of the Corebus/Celanta courtship. If we are shown Huanebango and Zantippa meeting (658 ff.), why do we not have a parallel situation with the other pair? In addition, all these lovers' stories drop from the action, as does the character Lampriscus. Why are they not brought into the *dénouement* (p. 179)?
4. The ending is especially huddled. 'Delia . . . hails [Eumenides] as her rescuer and the deliverer of her brothers without having been told anything of what has happened' (p. 179). Erestus and Venelia are restored to each other without either speaking a word (p. 180).[39]

To deal first with the argument that the play's brevity indicates cutting. S. Musgrove, in answer to Jenkins, suggests that the play was not intended as a full-length work, but as a light-hearted afterpiece, following a serious romantic comedy—and that the occasion for a 'double bill' of this nature would most likely be a private, rather than a public performance.[40] Jenkins assumes that the Queen's Men's performances in the provinces (*c*. 1590+) were the result of their declining fortunes, but accounts of their activities show that from 1583 on, they were annually spending many months travelling, sometimes acting in inns, sometimes in noblemen's houses.[41] The accounts suggest that the company performed other short plays. A troupe that performed *more* in the country (and sometimes at court) than in

London theatres need not mainly have presented two-and-a-half-hour plays. *The Old Wives Tale* could have been always brief. Nor need it necessarily have been an afterpiece, but simply a short work written for private performance, for some special occasion—perhaps a marriage?

There are several things about the play that give indication of private performance: the 'Lylian' language of the Pages in the opening, the intellectual humour in the literary parodies of the Huanebango/Zantippa episode, the frequent masquing elements (the prominence of music, the dances of the Harvesters (259.1, 560.1), the magical 'discovery' of Delia (880.1)). Even though there are episodes of broad comedy (the churchyard scene at 474 ff., the quarrel between the two sisters at 648 ff.) the overall tone of the play is sophisticated.

There is, in addition, something about the mood of the play that makes the thought that it was written for a marriage entertainment attractive. Its central theme—the quest for love and the jubilation at its discovery—is common to all dramatic romance, but the presentation of the theme in an atmosphere often resembling that of courtly entertainment makes it easy to imagine *The Old Wives Tale* as a gracious compliment and marriage gift. Indeed, the play can be said essentially to be about 'giving': from Clunch's initial gift of hospitality, to Madge's tale, through the various gestures of kindness and magnanimity in the action, to the last gift of all—the play itself as a wedding present to the lovers the celebration honours.[42] One can see the play, with its own kind of unity and integrity, as a brief entertainment, rather than as a cut-down version of a longer play.

But, while acknowledging the relative brevity, one must also keep in mind that the action takes more time to perform than a mere reading would indicate. In common with masques and entertainments, it impresses through visual means fully as much as verbal. Venelia's entrance 'madding all enraged' (201.1), Sacrapant's conjuring to please Delia (385 ff.), the songs and dances of the Harvesters (259.1, 560.1), the episode of the Fiddlers at the inn (767.1–2), the magical rising of the Heads from the well (663.1, 813.1), Jack's destruction of the symbols of

Sacrapant's power (846.1 ff.), Venelia's breaking the glass and blowing out the light (875.2), the 'discovery' of Delia (880.1)—all take time to stage, and these moments of music and mime are no less important than the spoken dialogue. Even though *The Old Wives Tale* may be shorter than many comedies, in performance it is not unduly brief.

To turn now to the specific incidents which Jenkins lists in support of his theory that the play is a cut version: (1) Erestus' 'Was she fair?' (see p. 13, above).

If one enters the world of *The Old Wives Tale* as naturally as Fantastic and Frolic enter the world of Madge's tale, especially heeding her admonition, 'Nay, either hear my tale, or kiss my tail' (120), it is obvious that the level on which the play is working is that of basic myth, folklore, and legend. This is not to say that it is 'simple-minded'; if the audience, upon seeing it, re-enters the realm of childhood, it does so with adult understanding and 'knows the place for the first time'. A sensibility attuned to the worth of a recovery of innocence would see Erestus' sudden, illogical response to the Brothers as a high moment of emotive and mythic power, rather than as a lacuna in the text.[43] Gummere's annotation on the line seems to grasp the significance of what is happenening: 'Erestus, who . . . "speaks in riddles", knows the errand of the Brothers, and asks the question abruptly.' Schelling's comment, as well, seems astute: 'he knows their errand without being told'. Whether anything has dropped from the text or not, still, the moment, as it stands, is one of the finest in the play.[44]

(2) Sacrapant's words to the Friar, 'Hold thee there, friar!' (410), do not necessarily indicate interruption of a now vanished diatribe against usurers. Hook interprets Sacrapant as saying, 'Hold fast to that opinion.' Such a reading has the advantage of revealing an irony: Sacrapant's agreement with the Friar is an example of the pot calling the kettle black. Sacrapant may agree with the Friar's condemnation of usury, but sorcerers are deeper in hell than usurers, and their corruption of nature is more serious (see Dante, *Inferno*, XVII, 43–75). Nor does the brevity of the Friar's appearance necessarily indicate cutting.

Such appearances are a norm in the action (see particularly the entrances of the Brothers and the Furies in the episode immediately following (414–40)) and are also part of the essential fabric of folk tales, by nature episodic and filled with sudden encounters.

(3) That the audience sees Huanebango and Zantippa meeting, but not Corebus and Celanta, is rather an example of dramatic economy than evidence of cutting. One knows naturally, from the laws governing the telling of tales, that to see one pair is to imagine both. The comic lovers' stories (and Lampriscus) drop from the action not because the resolution of their tales is missing but because it is not necessary that they be completed. One knows perfectly well that Lampriscus is happy and that the two comic marriages are exactly appropriate. If the *dénouement* seems to Jenkins 'huddled' as the quarto gives it to us, how much more huddled would it appear if Lampriscus, Huanebango, Corebus, Zantippa, and Celanta were dragged in.

(4) Delia's immediate recognition of Eumenides is, like Erestus' sudden question 'Was she fair?', wholly acceptable, and, indeed, fitting, on the level of imaginative tale-telling. What is rationally incredible is emotionally and mythically authentic. The prominence of 'irrational' moments is the play's strength, not its flaw. Similarly, that Erestus and Venelia do not speak when reunited is rather *coup de théâtre* than evidence of mangled text.

The strongest point in Jenkins's thesis is his discussion of the Booby/Corebus crux. Jenkins argues that the first Huanebango scene (264.1–351) was to be cut, in the version prepared for the provinces. It is a survival from the original, longer text; and its presence in Q. is a result of the printer not following deletion marks. Madge introduces Huanebango twice (266 and 566). If the first scene were omitted, the redundancy would vanish. The character 'Booby' in the first Huanebango scene is likewise evidence that the scene is a remnant from an earlier, extended version. Originally, the play contained two characters: 'Booby', the Clown of 265–351 (who is identical to the 'Corebus' in later scenes (564.1 ff.)), and the 'Corebus' of the churchyard episode

(474–553). When the first Huanebango scene was cut, the parts of Corebus-friend-of-Jack and Corebus Huanebango's servant were merged. For reasons of economy, one actor could play both.[45] Jenkins also contrasts the style of the first Huanebango scene with that in the second brief appearance of Huanebango and Corebus (565–92), where the pair is struck deaf and blind by Sacrapant. With the first scene 'the writer revels in its comedy and has time to elaborate a little his comic idea. But nowhere else outside the induction does he do this' (p. 183).

Jenkins's argument is attractive and important, since it logically accounts for the most difficult of the play's textual problems. But for the appearance of the 'two' Clowns in the play, the whole theory that the quarto text preserves an abridged version might never have arisen. Yet while the crux does indicate that something has gone amiss, there are points to be raised against Jenkins's interpretation, and there may be a simpler cause for the confusion.

It is true that Madge introduces Huanebango twice, but this double introduction is, as with other incidents, in accord with the methods of tale-telling. Peele consciously makes use of repetition, and recurring phrases become formulaic. When Madge asks concerning Huanebango, 'Who have we here?' (565), it does not mean that the earlier introduction, and scene, should be omitted. Hers is a rhetorical, ritual question, recalling the idiom of old tales. 'Who have we here?' is asked many times (see 143, 257, 559). As Hook says, 'Redundancy is the rule in the play' (p. 347). For instance, Sacrapant's introduction of the Brothers at 441–2, and his description of their mission ('to seek Delia their sister forth'), repeats what the First Brother has said at 135–9.

Instead of being superfluous, the first Huanebango scene is vital to the play. It is in this scene that we hear the prophecy essential to the later development of the Huanebango plot:

> Thanks, son, but list to me:
> He shall be deaf when thou shalt not see.
> Farewell, my son; things may so hit,
> Thou mayst have wealth to mend thy wit. (346–9)

If the scene were meant to be cut, some version of this prophecy would have had to be included in the second Huanebango scene.

Jenkins is correct when he contrasts the 'leisurely' mood of the comedy of the first Huanebango scene with the rapid sequence of action of the second appearance of Huanebango and Corebus (when Sacrapant afflicts them). Yet he neglects to mention the third appearance of Huanebango, in the scene with Zantippa at the well (658–717). Here the comedy is as leisurely and sophisticated as in the first scene.[46] Both scenes are hilarious, but the level of foolery is not slapstick. The first scene builds on the questing knight and braggart soldier types, makes some jokes in Latin, parodies Plautus and satirises 'first families'. The scene with Zantippa (eight lines *longer* than the first) parodies romantic unions, takes time for the chant of the Head in the well (a moment at once funny and entrancing), parodies a poem by Gabriel Harvey, Stanyhurst's translation of *Aeneid*, and courtly love poems ('Her silver teeth', etc.), and, like the earlier scene, ends with a jibe at people's pride in their pedigrees. Surely here 'outside the induction' the writer 'has time to elaborate a little his comic idea'. Corebus is not in the scene, and it is perhaps for this reason that Jenkins does not deal with it. But it would seem that if abridgement was the object, there is much here that could be cut.

Finally, the Booby/Corebus confusion may be accounted for differently from Jenkins's view. Hook regards it, convincingly I think, as further evidence that the printer's copy was authorial. As so great a confusion of *dramatis personae* would not appear in a polished form of the manuscript, we can assume 'something earlier than a final draft' (p. 348), very foul papers. Peele 'started with Booby, the traditional name for a fool. When he introduced Corebus-friend-of-Jack . . . he remembered from his school days that Corebus was also a fool and decided to use the name for the Clown, probably intending to make changes that would eliminate the confusion' (p. 348). The implication here is that Peele intended for Huanebango's servant and the Corebus of the churchyard scene to remain two different characters; yet it is also possible to imagine that Peele began with the clown Booby, then developed a separate character (Corebus-friend-of-Jack), and then decided to merge the two characters, but neglected to change Booby's name.[47] The advantage of having one Clown is that Corebus, in the churchyard scene, provides a link between the romantic love story and the Huanebango comic action. Huanebango's servant is also a friend of Jack, Eumenides' ghostly helper.

The case for foul papers in an early state must remain a hypothesis until clearer evidence is found. The only autograph MS of Peele's to survive is *Anglorum Feriae*,[48] but comparison of its spelling peculiarities with those of *The Old Wives Tale* does not take one very far. Frequently, in *Anglorum Feriae* 'o' is doubled: coorts (7, 8, 92, 335),[49] swoorde (78), coorses (225), coorser (256), woorthy (312). *The Old Wives Tale*, however, has few such spellings, and the ones that appear are common to many early texts: dooes (does, 85), doo (do, 112, 123, 254, 291, 334),[50] foorth (forth, 274). Both works show incidents of 'i' being replaced by 'y' (*Ang. Fer.*: ycie (31, 290), yf (212, 269), fayntinge (278), yll (280). *O.W.T.*: yvorie (ivory, 157), foyson (foison, 338).) But the occurrences in *The Old Wives Tale* are too few to build much of a case on. In *The Old Wives Tale* quarto 'i' frequently replaces 'e': inough (322), inchaunting (367), incounter (691), indure (866), inhansing (892); but *Anglorum Feriae* offers no such spellings.

In his introduction to Peele's *The Arraignment of Paris*, R. M. Benbow concludes that the printer's copy for the work was 'closely related to the autograph manuscript'.[51] The stage directions are especially descriptive and leisurely, as befitting a text that intended to recreate in the reader's eye the original splendour of the courtly show. It is true that they resemble the style of stage directions in *The Old Wives Tale*, but, once more, the search for evidence other than stage directions does not yield much. A few spellings peculiar to *Anglorum Feriae* appear again in *The Arraignment of Paris*: e.g. dooble (92), simpathye (548). But there are not enough similarities for one to draw a firm conclusion. The most unusual words in *The Old Wives Tale* are 'quiners . . . quine', and perusal of *The Arraignment* gives one 'quier' for 'choir' (166 S.D.); but 'quier' is more common than 'quine' and not especially peculiar to Peele.

It would therefore seem that the exact nature of the printer's copy may never be known. If it represents a cut version, it is well cut—one might conjecture by Peele himself, rather than by a hack. The case for the quarto being printed from foul papers has been shown, but the evidence is not as plentiful as one might wish.

SOURCES

In a sense, everything is a source for *The Old Wives Tale*, while its actual direct sources are few and relatively insignificant. All literature has myth, folk tales and legend at its core, but in *The Old Wives Tale* Peele consciously recreates the basic aim of folklore—to recall to the hearer the instincts and images of his childhood and to reawaken in him a sense of surprise, mystery, and wonder.

As an example of how the sources for *Old Wives Tale* are simultaneously specific and universal, one can look at the relationship between the play and one of its sources, Apuleius' *The Golden Ass*. Peele may have taken the name Meroe (Sacrapant's mother (358)) and the Thessalonian setting (357, 441, 620, 954) from the prose romance; yet beyond these concrete but minor connections, one discovers a more vital resemblance.[52] The narrator of *The Golden Ass* declares that his tales are:

> stories of men's forms and fortunes transformed into different shapes, and then restored again in due sequence back into their selves—a true subject for wonder.[53]

Peele's tale is about metamorphosis, and so designed as to transform the perception of the audience, as the action moves from a rational world to one of enchantment. Within the tale, Erestus is changed into a bear and an old man; Venelia into a mad, mute woman; Sacrapant transformed himself into a dragon, then into a seeming youth; Jack appears to be a live man—and, at the end, all original forms are restored. Beyond these incidents in Madge's tale, a higher level of metamorphosis develops. Antic and Fantastic, and the audience, see fiction become reality: 'Soft, gammer, here some come to tell your tale for you' (133). In the end, it is much more than the characters within the play who are 'restored to their former liberty' (879). Fantastic and Antic began by being 'lost in the woods' (3) and end by being awakened into wonder, as is, of course, the audience.[54]

Although all folklore, in general, may be part of the background for *The Old Wives Tale* (Peele at times seeming to fill the action as full as possible with fragments of countless tales and innumerable motifs), one can, nevertheless, point to a few specific tales which Peele draws on. Two tales definitely reworked into the fabric of the plot are 'The Grateful Dead' and 'The Three Heads of the Well'. There are, in addition, some tales less crucial to the action from which Peele has used motifs and episodes: 'Childe Roland', 'The Red Ettin', and 'Jack the Giant-killer'.

The ancient story of 'The Grateful Dead' has many variants, but essentially tells of the hero who, like Eumenides, pays 'for the burying of a poor fellow' (946–7) and is rewarded for his generosity by the ghost of the dead man.[55] Peele seems to have drawn on the version which unites the basic story with the tales of 'The Ransomed Woman' and 'The Water of Life'. In the first, the hero is reunited with his beloved through the benificence of the ghost, and, in the second, princely brothers quest for healing water, which the youngest (with supernatural assistance) obtains, whereupon he releases his enchanted brothers (or sister).

It is immediately apparent that Peele has complicated and rearranged the stories. *The Old Wives Tale* has several questors: Erestus (whose reunion with Venelia seems to come from 'The Ransomed Woman'), the Two Brothers (related to the princes of 'The Water of Life'), Eumenides (from the simplest form of 'The Grateful Dead'), and Huanebango (a parody of the others). At the same time, Peele unites the theme of 'The Water of Life' with the story of 'The Three Heads of the Well'.[56] In this tale, two daughters (one ugly and bad-tempered, the other beautiful and kind) go out to seek husbands. The first daughter rejects an old beggar's supplication for food, but the second daughter responds to his plea. In return, he gives her advice on what to do when she comes to a magic well, out of which rise, one after the other, three Golden Heads, each one singing:

> Wash men, and comb me,
> And lay me down softly.
> And lay me on a bank to dry,
> That I may look pretty,
> When somebody passes by.[57]

The beautiful sister obeys the Heads and is rewarded with a princely husband. The ugly sister strikes the heads (*O.W.T.*, 674.1) and is thrice cursed: with leprosy, a harsh voice, and a poor country cobbler for a husband.

The Huanebango/Corebus/Zantippa/Celanta action derives from this tale, but one notices the witty alterations Peele has made. Zantippa may be fair, but she is a shrew; yet even with her bad temper she finds an oddly appropriate husband. Deaf Huanebango cannot hear her harsh voice, and she plans to give that braggart what he deserves by cuckolding him. It is the ugly Celanta who is kind to the Heads (two, in Peele's version), and she finds a fit mate in Corebus, who, being blind, cannot see her ugliness. Corebus' lack of brains is compensated for: 'thou mayst have wealth to mend thy wit' (349).

No sooner has one told the tales that form the main folklore sources for *The Old Wives Tale* than other stories having similar motifs come to mind. In 'Childe Roland', Burd Ellen, sister of the 'questing brothers', vanishes, carried off by servants of the King of Elfland.[58] Seeking her, the brothers go to Merlin for advice. Gummere and Crow find a link between Erestus and Merlin, in that Merlin likewise was a wise man appearing in the shape of a bear.[59] The 'Fee, fi, fo, fum' refrain (*O.W.T.*, 571) appears in 'Childe Roland'.[60]

'The Red Ettin' contains many motifs and episodes found in *The Old Wives Tale*. The younger of two brothers goes in search of the elder, who has been captured by the Red Ettin (a monstrous bull). He enters a castle and 'there he saw an old wife sitting beside the kitchen fire. He asked the wife if he might stay the night.'[61] The hero gives part of his cake to the old woman, and she, in return, provides him with forecasts and advice, which help him free his brother and win a king's daughter. Sacrapant's 'life index' (the light in a glass, which lasts as long as his life and skill) appears in the story in the form of a glowing knife, that fades when the elder brother is turned into a pillar of stone. The riddling motif ('she that's neither wife, widow nor maid' (449), 'never to die, but by a dead man's hand' (451)) occurs in 'The Red Ettin' when the monster asks the brothers such things as 'The dead carry the living: riddle me that.'

In 'Jack the Giant-killer' the hero is very much like Peele's Jack—a clever, tricky lad. The 'fee, fi, fo, fum' refrain likewise appears in the tale.[62]

It is impossible to say with certainty whether Peele was thinking specifically of these stories. The important thing to notice is that the manner in which he selects and moulds themes common to innumerable folk tales creates an effect of fantasy intentionally 'playing with' its own techniques and devices.

In addition to folk tales, there are a few literary sources for the play. That Peele probably derived some of his material from Greene's *Orlando Furioso* and Apuleius' *Golden Ass* has already been mentioned. Greene's romance *Perimedes the Blacksmith* (1588) shares with *The Old Wives Tale* the device of a frame story setting off the main action, and in Greene's work the frame itself bears a resemblance to the situation at the beginning of *The Old Wives Tale*: Perimedes, like Clunch, is a smith, and he and his wife pass away the time by tale-telling.[63] Schelling suggests that Peele may have taken the name Erestus from *Soliman and Perseda* (*c.* 1590), where we find a character 'Erastus',[64] but the plays have nothing else in common. One might just as well cite *The Spanish Tragedy* (*c.* 1587), in which 'Erastus' (or 'Erasto') is a character in Hieronimo's play.

A quasi-literary source for *The Old Wives Tale* may be the Harvey/Nashe quarrel. Gabriel Harvey had a reputation for

arrogance and pedantry, and antagonised younger wits, like
Robert Greene and Thomas Nashe. Greene's *A Quip for an
Upstart Courtier* (1592) and Nashe's *Pierce Penniless* (1592)
ridiculed Harvey, and he retaliated with *Foure Letters* (1592),
reviling Greene's supposedly licentious life, and attacking
Nashe. Nashe replied with *Foure Letters Confuted* (1593) and
*Have-with-you to Saffron-Walden, or Gabriel Harvey's Hunt is
Up* (1596). The theory that Peele joined with Nashe in the
quarrel by making Huanebango a parody of Harvey was first
proposed by Fleay in *A Biographical Chronicle of the English
Drama* (1891), II, p. 155.[65] It is only fairly recently that this view
has been discarded in favour of the idea that the inspiration for
Huanebango lies elsewhere.[66]

The link between *The Old Wives Tale* and folklore is so
obvious that it seems strange that no one before Muriel Bradbrook looked to folk plays as providing a source for the character
of Huanebango. Miss Bradbrook noted that Huanebango (with
his bragging cry of 'Fee, fa, fum' and his two-hand sword) seems
close kin to Bold Slasher and other giants of folk plays.[67]
Huanebango's comic 'resurrection' from the well (674.2)
appears to have behind it the sudden revivals of characters in
mummer's plays. In *The Revesby Sword Play* the Fool bounces
back to life,[68] and the Doctor's restoration of St George is a
recurring event.[69] The following episode from the *Oxfordshire St
George Play* is not unrelated to the action and tone of *The Old
Wives Tale*:

> *Enter Giant Blunderbore:*
> I am giant Blunderbore, fee, fi fum!
> Ready to fight ye all,—so I says 'Come!'
> *Enter Little Jack:*
> And this here is my little man Jack.
> A thump on his rump, and a whack on his back.[70]

Mumming, masquing, spectacle, and 'entertainment' appear
the natural parents of *The Old Wives Tale*. Peele preserves and
infuses with new energy the mood and purpose of these jubilant
celebrations of fertility.

CRITICAL VIEW

Something about *The Old Wives Tale*—perhaps because of the very fact that it is so brief and 'simple' (if a fairy tale is simple), and also perhaps because it rapidly juxtaposes so many varied conventions of legend, romance, and satire—has made critical appraisals of the play's nature achieve intense polarity. The view that the quarto is a 'mangled corpse' at least implies that Peele knew what he was doing, though we have only the sad remnants. Contrary to this is an attitude which one might call the 'wood-notes wild' theory—that the text gives us what Peele planned, but that he wrote unconsciously, out of *furor poeticas*, under the power of the irrational muse of folklore. John Crow, for instance, finds *The Old Wives Tale* completely confusing:

> I can see no possible way of explaining anything except on the assumption that this play is utterly and completely unsophisticated. . . . My suggestion is that Peele had in his mind a number of odds and ends of folklore, scraps from a variety of stories, and that he wove them together without really knowing at all what odd end came from what story. You will observe that he shows every sign of putting in a number of things that have a significance for us and had apparently no significance for him.[71]

Although Crow's theory that Peele was naive and unaware ends in this gross absurdity, it is one way of answering a view of the play at one time prevalent—that *The Old Wives Tale* does not use folklore seriously, but rather creates a satire of its own plot and convention. One can find the seed of the 'satire' idea in F. B. Gummere's introduction to the play. His essay is sensitive and subtle, the first criticism of the play to attempt to make more than a superficial examination of its tone and effect, but Gummere's conclusion is that Peele's chief aim (and accomplishment) was creating a special 'sense of humour':

> not the classical humour of *Roister Doister*, not the hearty but clumsy mirth of *Gammer Gurton*, but rather a hint of the extravagant and romantic which turns upon itself with audible merriment at its own pretences . . .[72]

Muriel Bradbrook observes that 'the view that *The Old Wives*

Tale was satiric or burlesque is now fairly generally discarded'.[73] The direction of criticism, since Gwenan Jones's important article 'The Intention of Peele's *Old Wives Tale*',[74] has been towards describing the play's unique, rich and strange blending of moods and episodes, and relating this atmosphere to that of other kinds of romances. Ironically, recent favourable critical attitudes are related to Crow's disparaging remarks:

> Peele could hardly have done better in the making of a strange jumble of folk stories if he had been a present-day scholar who had read all the folk stories of the world and written a play out of them in a dream.[75]

What Crow considers flaws may be the essence of the play's power: 'jumble', 'dream'. The basic method of tale-telling is often to create a 'jumble'—an irrational succession of events, surprise happenings, sudden reversals, intense conflation and 'huddling' at the tale's conclusion. What the method accomplishes is to recreate the quality of dream. Daylight 'reality' is suspended, and, as in the moonlit midsummer woods outside Athens, illogic and confusion bring emotional truth and order.

Gwenan Jones, in countering the view that *The Old Wives Tale* is a parody of romance (and, also, that it is 'straight' romance), stresses its relation to old tales:

> Peele has given us not the high-flowing tale of romantic adventure, but the familiar nursery tale, and has used something of the style as well as the material of the old wife.[76]

Thorleif Larsen, acknowledging that Miss Jones anticipated his views,[77] likewise stresses the resemblance between Madge's 'style and material' and that of fairy tales. The play's 'naïveté' and 'simplicity' are strengths, not weaknesses:

> In writing nursery rhymes, [Peele] has accomplished one of the most difficult things in the world.[78]

Writing a good nursery rhyme, as with a good children's book (witness James Thurber, E. B. White, Maurice Sendak) is difficult because in doing so one brings coherently to the conscious world the substance of fantasy and dream. The fragile territory created is 'the peculiar twilight between dreaming and waking.'[79] As Fantastic well knew, tales and dreams have something in common: 'I'faith, gammer, a tale of an hour long were as good as an hour's sleep.'

But to recognise that Peele uses the material and methods of folk tales does not go far enough toward describing the special qualities of *The Old Wives Tale*. One has not adequately answered the question about what effect the play has on the audience. If part of the effect is establishing a dreamlike quality, one must still ask further: '*Why* is Fantastic right? What happens (in the drama and in the audience) when a tale becomes 'as good as sleep'?

Herbert Goldstone works towards answering the question when he writes of what he considers the effect of Peele's world of 'jumble'—which, from a more favourable vantage point, can be called a world of interplay:

> . . . the ordinary and the fantastic, the strange and the everyday, can somehow be part of a unified whole. In short, Peele in *The Old Wives Tale* is really dramatising by means of interplay the working of the imagination and showing how it enlarges, unifies, and yet refreshingly complicates human life.[80]

The words are rhapsodic, but perhaps they are so because they attempt to describe the nebulous realm peculiar to dramatic romance, where art and nature, dream and waking, merge. The statue moves; Prospero's magic isle is at the same time our natural earth.

Muriel Bradbrook, thinking possibly along the same lines, puts more concretely what she finds the effect of Peele's use of folklore themes and methods to be. In *The Old Wives Tale*, as in tales one has known from childhood, and as in dreams, the everyday is merged with the fantastic; reversal and surprise are the essential dramatic idiom:

> the fluid of life of such plays (like ballads) belongs within folk tradition, where the marvelous must always be familiar, though it cannot be rational. Recognition of the familiar and delight by the unexpected must be evenly balanced for the audience to be 'rapt'.[81]

But *The Old Wives Tale* is not exactly the same as a nursery rhyme. If it is like old tales in providing the audience with the beneficial properties of fancy and dream, it is unlike them in that the audience is discouraged from identifying with the world of enchantment. That the audience be aware of the artifice is so important that Peele uses two means of removing the viewers from the action of Madge's story. First, through the frame story: the quest for Delia and Huanebango's parody quest are seen from the point of view of the old wife and her guests. Their comments interrupt the action and remind us that this is not 'life'. Secondly, the action within Madge's tale itself does not allow the audience to remain on one plane of perception. The Huanebango action mocks the main love story, but when the Eumenides action comes to the fore, it is not to be ridiculed. The 'jumble' at the ending makes it impossible for the audience to enter one realm of mood and feeling without being made suddenly to readjust its perspective. Jack cuts in on Sacrapant's finely histrionic death speech with a wry 'O sir, are you gone? Now I hope we shall have some other coil' (854–5). Then it is Jack himself who changes the mood to one of wonder when he draws the curtain *and there* DELIA *sitteth asleep*' (880.1). After the intentionally stylised reunion scene, Jack suddenly *'leaps down in the ground'* (950.1), and Eumenides immediately takes over Jack's role of wry commentator: 'Jack, what, art thou gone? Then, farewell, Jack' (951).

This revelation of artifice is part of the nature of dramatic romance. Even in early gallimaufries, like *Clyomon and Clamydes* (c. 1570), the presence of the Vice makes the audience reappraise its view of the main action, as Jack and Eumenides do at the *dénouement* of *The Old Wives Tale*.

What Peele's method accomplishes is to give the audience a sense of enlargement and freedom. The viewer is simultaneously connected with the magical heart of romance and legend (the main action of *The Old Wives Tale* is never made ludicrous) and made aware of the ordering and controlling hand of art. To the degree that he sympathises with the serious action, he becomes 'a child again', but, to the degree that he understands the purpose of the distancing effects, he is a judging adult. The viewer is healed by watching the play, for these parts of his nature are united.

So Fantastic speaks truly when he declares that a 'tale of an hour long were as good as an hour's sleep'. Indeed, dramatic romance has always aimed to bring healing and freedom. Caliban's exultant hope for 'freedom, hey-day, freedom!' is more soberly, but no less earnestly, expressed by Prospero's concluding prayer. In *The Winter's Tale*, Leontes is released from bondage to past guilt; Perdita and Florizel awaken into love.

If *The Old Wives Tale* was a wedding gift, the finest thing it bestowed upon the marriage couple and the rest of the audience was its power to release and restore—to make possible the return to one's most natural instincts of a child, while at the same time allowing one to re-experience these with conscious artistic awareness.

STAGE HISTORY

After its production in *c.* 1593, nothing is known about the stage history of *The Old Wives Tale* until modern times. Felix E. Schelling finds little in the play to merit its continued performance, but notes:

> It would not be surprising if the movies were some day to discover it. It has long been one of the most popular features of 'Big May Day', a pageant given every four years by the students of Bryn Mawr College [Pennsylvania, U.S.A.].[82]

Thomas Marc Parrott likewise mentions the Bryn Mawr performances, in a similarly condescending tone:

> The action [of *O.W.T.*] is a tangled web, a little difficult to follow in reading, a sheer delight when played in the open by a troupe of pretty girls at a Bryn Mawr May Day.[83]

All the modern revivals which I have been able to trace have been, indeed, performed by students—but, of course, it is obvious that the play's appropriateness as a vehicle for young actors does not derive from anything puerile or 'cute' about the work, but from its enchanting and mysterious revelation of the ground of fairy tale. The young, who are themselves close to the essential spirit of the play, can lead their elders to rediscover this spirit in themselves.[84]

The May Day performances at Bryn Mawr were in 1910, 1914, 1924, and 1928.[85] In 1919 and 1930 the play was produced by Marjorie Danns for the Literary Society of Birkbeck College, University of London. The past fifteen years have seen several revivals. On 29, 30 June 1962, Derek Forbes, Head of the Department of Drama Studies at Middlesex Polytechnic, produced an open-air performance in a sunken garden at Balls Park Training College, Hertfordshire. David Blostein produced the play twice: in 1963 at the University of Western Ontario (Huron College) and in 1969 at Victoria College, University of Toronto. G. B. Shand's production was given at York University, Toronto, in 1972. Richard Proudfoot directed a performance at King's College, London, on 25 June 1974. [86]

These recent performances have all used a *mise en scène* that does not rely on shifting scenery, but which works on the idea of a single set, comprised of several 'houses', which seems most likely to be the method Peele originally intended. The Well, Erestus' Cross, Sacrapant's Study, the Hill with its hidden light—all are fixed places, and the action moves from one *domus* to the next. Madge and the two pages remain on stage throughout. This arrangement permits the audience to perceive, despite rapid shifts in setting and the appearance of many varied characters, an underlying unity in the action of *The Old Wives Tale*.

NOTES TO INTRODUCTION

1 See 'Authorship and Date'.
2 For details on what we know of Peele's life, see Cheffaud and Horne.
3 See Horne, p. 59.
4 Intro., p. 1. Hook gives the following details on the 'subscriptions': 'It accompanies his name on the title pages of the printed versions of *A Farewell* (1589), *An Eclogue Gratulatory* (1589), *Descensus Astraeae* (1591), *The Honour of the Garter* (1593), and the second edition of *A Tale of Troy* (1604); on the verso side of the title page of *Polyhymnia* (1590); and . . . on the title page of the holograph of *Anglorum Feriae* (1595).'
5 Horne, p. 43.
6 *Ibid.*, p. 65.

7 See pp. 5, 23–4.

8 *Groats-worth of Wit*, ed. G. B. Harrison (Edinburgh, 1966), p. 45.

9 Greg's 'new vampt' version of the play calls the quarto 'no more than a mangled corpse' (p. 3).

10 Oral comment in a lecture on Principles of Literary Criticism, Toronto, 1960. Quoted by permission.

11 *Elizabethan Plays* (London, 1934), Intro., p. v.

12 Vol. II, p. 441.

13 Hook, p. 303. The scope of this introduction does not permit lengthy discussion of the history of attribution of *O.W.T.* to Peele. Those interested in details should consult Thorleif Larsen, 'The Growth of the Peele Canon', *The Library*, Fourth Series, XI, pp. 301, 304–6; and Hook's Introduction, pp. 303–5.

14 Consider the variety of genres in the Peele canon: miscellaneous poems, mainly on classical subjects; pageants; *The Arraignment of Paris* (pastoral); *David and Bethsabe* (biblical history); *Edward I* (English historical romance); *The Battle of Alcazar* (foreign historical romance and adventure).

15 Hook, p. 304. Additional examples are cited.

16 *Ibid.*, pp. 304–5.

17 E. K. Chambers, *The Elizabethan Stage*, II, p. 114.

18 *Idem*. Chambers quotes the entry in Henslowe's *Diary* (8 May 1594) in which Henslowe notes a loan of £15 from his nephew Francis 'to lay downe for his share to the Quenes players when they broke & went into the country to playe'. (But the fact that the Queen's Men were acting in the provinces does not in itself provide any clue as to whether perhaps *O.W.T.* represents a cut version prepared for country audiences.)

19 The passages are quoted at 686–7n. and 890–3n.

20 See *Orlando*, ll. 90–6: 'And what I dare, let say the Portingale, / And Spaniard tell, who mand with mighty Fleetes, / Came to subdue my Ilands to their King, / Filling our Seas with stately Argosies, / Calvars and Magars, hulkes of burden great, / Which Brandemart rebated from his coast, / And sent them home ballast with little wealth.' (*Malone Society Reprints*, 1907). *Orlando* was entered in the *Stationer's Register* on 7 December 1593 and 28 May 1594. The quarto appeared in 1594. The date of composition is uncertain: *c.* 1592?

21 See 676, 689nn.

22 Muriel Bradbrook explores this idea in 'Peele's *Old Wives Tale*: a Play of Enchantment', *English Studies*, XLIII (1962), pp. 323–30. See p. 24.

23 *A Transcript of the Registers of the Company of Stationers of London: 1554–1640*, ed. Edward Arber (London, 1875), II, p. 296.

24 See, however, 327–8n.

25 The following three paragraphs were written in close consultation with the general editor, and several points are his.

26 The printer John Danter has a reputation for producing inferior printings of pirated works (see E. K. Chambers, *The Elizabethan Stage*, III, p. 187, and R. B. McKerrow, *A Dictionary of Printers and Booksellers in England . . .*, pp. 83–4). He printed the Bad Quarto of *Romeo and Juliet* in 1597. Yet *The Old Wives Tale* does not at all resemble a bad quarto, either in text or in specific details of printing; and the 1594 quarto of *Titus Andronicus* is good.

27 The one exception is C1v (twenty-eight lines).

28 Hook, p. 381.

29 So Hook, p. 378. See also 825n.

30 In today's usage, both a cornerstone and a keystone are called quoins; but, earlier, a quoin could mean 'coin' (money) as well. See *O.E.D.*

31 See 665n.

32 On D4v, S.H. for Celanta is a careless '*Clant.*'. See also 803.1n. on Celanta/ Zelanto readings.

33 Hook points out that 'descry' is repeated immediately in the dialogue: 'Stay, brother! What hast thou descried?' (630). He considers the duplication 'clear indication of the author' (p. 351).

34 So reads the direction in Q. The entrances of the two men are separated in this edition.

35 Of course, if the play is staged by having separate 'houses' (Sacrapant's cave, Erestus' cross, etc.), Erustus has never actually left the stage, but has retired to his *domus*. Hence a formal '*Enter* ERESTUS' is not obligatory. See 'Stage History', and 249n.

36 I here concur with Hook, pp. 351–4.

37 One further possibility, that Q. was printed from an unauthorised report of the play, cannot for long be seriously considered. The play is too finely wrought.

38 *Modern Language Review*, XXXIV, 1934, pp. 177–85. Muriel Bradbrook (*op. cit.*, p. 323) says that it is 'clear that the play has been shortened'.

39 Jenkins makes clear that his theory rests on cumulative evidence, not on any one point alone.

40 'Peele's *Old Wives Tale*: an Afterpiece?', *Journal of the Australasian Universities Language and Literature Association*, XXIII, 1965, pp. 89–95.

41 See Chambers, *op. cit.*, II, pp. 105–12.

42 I am indebted to G. B. Shand (York University, Toronto) for bringing to my attention the importance of the theme of giving.

43 While Hook disagrees with Jenkins that the quarto is a cut version, he nevertheless thinks that something has dropped out before 'Was she fair?', as a result of compositor's error (p. 345).

44 See also 158n.

45 Jenkins, pp. 182–4. Bradbrook (*op. cit.*, p. 325) considers the first Huanebango scene an accretion, added by popular demand.

46 Jenkins uses 'leisurely' to mean the amount of stage time the scene takes. In both scenes the mood and pace are not 'leisurely' in the sense of 'relaxed'.

47 As discussed above, pp. 11–12, the names of characters tend to be unfixed: Senex/Erestus, Old Woman/Madge, Churchwarden/Simon/Steven Loach.

48 See Yale Peele, I, p. 178.

49 Line numbers refer to Yale Peele text, ed. Horne.

50 The spelling is probably Compositor A's, at any rate. See p. 8.

51 Yale Peele, III, p. 54.

52 See Apuleius, p. 5, for the first mention of Thessaly. The story of Meroe begins on p. 13.

53 Apuleius, p. 3.

54 Margaret Dean-Smith, in 'Folk-play Origins of the English Masque',

Folk-Lore, LXV, 1954, speaks of the essence of folk tales as a celebration of rejuvenated nature (p. 79).

55 For an indication of how widespread the tale is, see G. K. Gerould's *The Grateful Dead* (London, 1908).

56 The tale is printed in *English Fairy Tales*, ed. Jospeh Jacobs (1890), pp. 222–7. Another version is entitled 'The Princess of Colchester'. See E. S. Hartland, *English Fairy and other Folk Tales* (1890) p. 20–4.

57 Jacobs, p. 223. Compare *O.W.T.*, 666–7, 814–15.

58 *Ibid.*, pp. 117–30.

59 See Gummere, p. 345, and John Crow, 'Folklore in Elizabethan Drama', *Folk-Lore*, LVIII, 1947, p. 305. Traditionally, Merlin was 'the last of England's bears'. See James T. Bracher, 'Peele's *Old Wives Tale* and Tale-Type 425A', in *Studies in Medieval, Renaissance, American Literature: A Festschrift*, ed. Betsy Fengan Colquitt. Fort Worth: Texas Christian University Press, 1971, pp. 95–102.

60 Jacobs, p. 123.

61 *Ibid.*, p. 133.

62 *Ibid.*, p. 109.

63 *Works*, ed. Grosart, VII, pp. 1–85. The old wife's name, in Greene's story, is Delia. This does not prove that Peele derived his Delia's name from Greene, for the name was a frequent one in romance. Yet, that the two works share the name may indicate a connection.

64 *Typical Elizabethan Plays*, p. 202.

65 Dyce had suggested earlier (1883 edition of *O.W.T.*, p. 342) that 'Peele intended to ridicule and mortify Harvey', but only at line 683, where Peele actually quotes Harvey's *Ecomium Lauri*. See 683n.

66 For the places in the text that prompted the identification of Harvey and Huanebango, see notes on 264.1, 270–1, 302–3, 571, 676, and 683. For a full account of the Harvey/Nashe quarrel, see Nashe, *Works*, V, pp. 65–110, and Hook (Intro., pp. 311–19).

67 Bradbrook, *op. cit.*, p. 328.

68 J. Q. Adams, *Chief Pre-Shakespearean Dramas* (1924), p. 361. The ensuing action is crammed with unmotivated entrances of dancers, and the characters 'Pickle Herring', 'Allspice', etc. This 'medley' action is similar to the sudden entrances in *O.W.T.* The 'resurrection' of Falstaff, that better-known braggart soldier (*1H4*, V.iv.111), may also have folk origins. This comparison with Falstaff can serve to point out the fallacy in equating Huanebango and Harvey. Huanebango's relation to Harvey is about the same as Falstaff's to Sir John Oldcastle..

69 See the *Leicestershire St George Play* (Adams, p. 356) and the *Oxfordshire St George Play* (Adams, p. 354).

70 Adams, p. 353.

71 Crow, *op. cit.*, p. 303. Blair's thesis also propounds this theory. One might note the paradox in the quotation from Crow: if Peele 'wove' we would infer a conscious skill.

72 Gummere, p. 338. Precisely what Gummere means is often elusive and his meanings difficult to penetrate: e.g. 'It is . . . a comedy of comedies, a saucy challenge of romance, where art turns, however timidly, upon itself' (p. 346). What Gummere calls 'sense of humour' is later defined more rigidly as

'burlesque'. See Thorleif Larsen, 'The Old Wives Tale by George Peele', Transactions of the Royal Society of Canada, XXIX (1935), pp. 157–70, for a full bibliography of the proponents of the 'satire' view. Larsen notes that Tucker Brooke, for instance, lists the play under 'Travesties of Heroic Plays'.

73 Bradbrook, op. cit., p. 324.

74 Aberystwyth Studies, VII (1925), pp. 79–93.

75 Crow, op. cit, p. 303.

76 Jones, op. cit., p. 88.

77 'The Old Wives Tale', p. 157n.

78 Ibid., p. 170.

79 Ibid., p. 162.

80 'Interplay in Peele's The Old Wives Tale', Boston University Studies in English, IV (1960), p. 213.

81 Bradbrook, op. cit., p. 325.

82 Typical Elizabethan Plays (1926), p. 203

83 A Short View of Elizabethan Drama (1943), p. 68. The programmes for Bryn Mawr's Big May Day show undertakings more ambitious than beauty pageants by troupes of pretty girls. In 1914 the programme consisted of Munday's The Downfall of Robert, Earl of Huntington and The Death of Robert, Earl of Huntington, Lyly's Campaspe, Peele's Old Wives Tale, Shakespeare's Midsummer Night's Dream, The Oxfordshire Play of St. George, The Revesby Sword Play, and the Chester Noah's Flood.

84 Both Derek Forbes and Richard Proudfoot, in describing their productions to me, said that they felt that the play may have been written for a boys' company, even though it became the property of the Queen's Men.

85 Gertrude Reed, Librarian of Bryn Mawr, kindly supplied me with the relevant programmes.

86 The Old Wives Tale was also broadcast over BBC radio, in the autumn of 1972.

THE OLD WIVES TALE

[DRAMATIS PERSONAE

ANTIC ⎫
FROLIC ⎬ *Pages*
FANTASTIC ⎭
CLUNCH, *A Smith*
MADGE, *the Old Wife*

FIRST BROTHER (Calypha) ⎫
SECOND BROTHER (Thelea) ⎬ *Brothers to Delia*
ERESTUS, *the Old Man at the Cross*
VENELIA, *his betrothed*
LAMPRISCUS
HUANEBANGO, *a Braggart Soldier*
COREBUS, *the Clown*
SACRAPANT, *the Conjurer*
DELIA
EUMENIDES, *the Wandering Knight*
WIGGEN
CHURCHWARDEN
SEXTON
ZANTIPPA, *the Curst Daughter* ⎫
CELANTA, *the Foul Wench* ⎬ *Daughters to Lampriscus*
JACK
HOSTESS
HEAD

Harvesters, Friar, Echo, two Furies, a Voice, Fiddlers]

Clunch] meaning a lumpish fellow—clodhopper, boor.

Erestus] See Intro., p. 23, for a possible source for the name.

Huanebango] Fleay (*A Biographical Chronicle of the English Drama*, II, p. 155) thought the name to be travestied from chivalric romance: Huon o' Bordeaux. Muriel Bradbrook ('Peele's *Old Wives Tale*: a Play of Enchantment', *English Studies*, XLIII, p. 328) suggests that the name is 'Juan y Bango', a type of the egotistic Spanish braggart, like Don Adriano de Armado in *L.L.L.*

Corebus] called *Booby* in the first Huanebango scene (264.1–351). For discussion of the Booby / Corebus crux, see Intro., pp. 10, 16–19. Corebus was a traditional name for a fool. Gummere sees in Peele's choice of name evidence that Huanebango is meant to be a parody of Gabriel Harvey, in that Harvey uses the name to mock Nashe: 'Thou mayest be cald the very Choroebus of our time, of whom the proverbe was sayde, more foole than Choroebus: who was a seely

The Old Wives Tale

Enter ANTIC, FROLIC, *and* FANTASTIC.

Antic. How now, fellow Frolic! What, all amort? Doth this
sadness become thy madness? What though we have
lost our way in the woods, yet never hang the head, as
though thou hadst no hope to live till tomorrow; for
Fantastic and I will warrant thy life tonight for   5
twenty in the hundred.

Frolic. Antic and Fantastic, as I am frolic franion, never in
all my life was I so dead slain. What? to lose our way
in the wood, without either fire or candle, so uncomfortable? *O coelum! O terra! O maria! O Neptune!*   10

---

1. Frolic] *Dyce; Franticke Q.*   9. candle,] *Dyce;* candle *Q.*   9–10. uncomfortable?] *Q.;* uncomfortable! *Neilson.*

---

ideot, but yet had the name of a wise man' (Harvey's *Have With you to Saffron-
Walden*, in Nashe, vol. V, p. 29).

Sacrapant] The conjurer's name is originally from Ariosto's *Orlando Furioso*
(Sacripante). In Robert Greene's *Orlando* it is spelled Sacripant. See Intro., p. 5.

Wiggen] The name is, as Hook notes, a variant of 'widgeon' a wild
duck—supposedly stupid—hence, a fool (*O.E.D.*).

Zantippa] Elizabethan form of Xanthippe, Socrates' wife—hence, allusively,
an ill-tempered woman. See First Folio text of *Shr.*, I.ii.71: 'As curst and
shrow'd / As *Socrates Zentippe*'.

1. *Frolic*] The emendation is called for, in view of 'Fantastic and I' (5). Also, if
the name is not emended, Frolic's play on his name (7) is lost.

all amort] from *à la mort*, *i.e.* mortally sick, dispirited, dejected. See *1H6*,
III.ii.124: 'What, all amort? Rouen hangs her head for grief.'

2. *madness*] levity.

5–6. *warrant . . . hundred*] the usual rate for travel insurance in Elizabethan
times. See Hook, p. 422.

7. *franion*] a gay, reckless fellow.

8. *dead slain*] exhausted, in the same sense as 'all amort' (1).

10. O coelum . . . Neptune] 'O heaven, earth, sea, Neptune'. Commonly
used expletive, derived from Terence's *Adelphoe* (IV, 790): '*O caelum, O terra, O
maria Neptuni!*'

Fantastic. Why makes thou it so strange, seeing Cupid
   hath led our young master to the fair lady, and she is
   the only saint that he hath sworn to serve?

Frolic. What resteth then but we commit him to his
   wench, and each of us take his stand up in a tree, and   15
   sing out our ill fortune to the tune of 'O man in
   desperation'?

Antic. Desperately spoken, fellow Frolic, in the dark: but
   seeing it falls out thus, let us rehearse the old
   proverb: [*Sings.*]   20

   Three merry men, and three merry men,
   And three merry men be we.
   I in the wood, and thou on the ground,
   And Jack sleeps in the tree.   [*A dog barks.*]

Fantastic. Hush! a dog in the wood, or a wooden dog! O   25
   comfortable hearing! I had even as lief the chamber-
   lain of the White Horse had called me up to bed.

S.H. 11. *Fantastic.*] (*Fantas.*) *not indented in* Q.   S.D. 24. *A dog barks*]
Hook.   S.H. 25. *Fantastic.*](*Fan.*) *not indented in* Q.   26. lief] (liue) Q.

---

11. *makes thou it*] behave you.

12. *young master*] probably a conscious preparation for the main theme of
Madge's tale. If the occasion for the play was a marriage feast, the line also
extends the action to another 'journey with Cupid', that of the 'young master'
and the 'fair lady' watching the play. The pages' young master never appears,
but there is a feeling that he is present, perhaps in the person of the bridegroom
in the audience.

16–17. *O man in desperation*] a well-known tune. See Nashe's *Summer's Last
Will and Testament* (III, p. 260).

20. S.D.] The song is probably sung as a round, Antic beginning.

21. Three merry men] another well-known tune. See the Variorum *Tw. N.*
(II.iii.69). Note that the pages sing a happy song, just after expressing a desire to
sing a doleful one. That they do so is in keeping with their characters.

24. Jack] 'Jack' actually appears later in the play. Much in the frame story is
taken up again when the tale begins: the bestowing of charity, the quest for love.

25. *wooden*] mad. See *M.N.D.*, II.i.192.

27. *White Horse*] a well-known London Tavern, in Friday Street. It is mentioned in *The Merry Conceited Jests of George Peele* (Bullen, II, p. 386).

Frolic. Either hath this trotting cur gone out of his circuit,
or else are we near some village,

    Enter [CLUNCH] *a Smith, with a lantern and candle.*

which should not be far off, for I perceive the glim'-   30
ring of a glow-worm, a candle, or a cat's eye, my life
for a halfpenny. In the name of my own father, be
thou ox or ass that appearest, tell us what thou art.
Clunch. What am I? Why, I am Clunch the smith. What
are you? What make you in my territories at this time   35
of the night?
Antic. What do we make dost thou ask? Why, we make
faces for fear; such as if thy mortal eyes could behold,
would make thee water the long seams of thy side
slops, smith.   40
Frolic. And in faith, sir, unless your hospitality do relieve
us, we are like to wander with a sorrowful heigh-ho,
among the owlets and hobgoblins of the forest. Good
Vulcan, for Cupid's sake that hath cozened us all,
befriend us as thou mayest, and command us how-   45
soever, wheresoever, whensoever, in whatsoever, for
ever and ever.
Clunch. Well, masters, it seems to me you have lost your
way in the wood. In consideration whereof, if you will
go with Clunch to his cottage, you shall have house-   50

S.D. 29.1] *as* Q.; *after* halfpenny 32, *Dyce; after* perceive, 30, *Neilson.*
CLUNCH] *Dyce 1861.*   S.H. 34. *Clunch.*] *Dyce 1861, passim; Smith. Q.*

---

34. *Clunch*] See *Dramatis Personae* n.
35. *What make you?*] What is your business?
39–40. *side slops*] wide, baggy breeches.
44. *Vulcan*] the god of smiths.
44–5. *for Cupid's sake . . . befriend us as thou mayest*] The lines are thematic to
the play as a whole.
45–7.] The contrast between the pages' extravagant rhetoric and Clunch's
simple answer (48–9) is highly comic. Gummere suggests that the pages' words
are a 'sort of parody on the appeal of wandering knights or travellers in
romances, and Clunch, with his "territories", may take the place of enchanter,
giant, or the like'.

room and a good fire to sit by, although we have no
bedding to put you in.

All. O blessed smith! O bountiful Clunch!

Clunch. For your further entertainment, it shall be as it
may be, so and so.   55

Here a dog barks.

Hark! this is Ball my dog, that bids you all welcome in
his own language. Come, take heed for stumbling on
the threshold. Open door, Madge; take in guests.

Enter [MADGE, *an*] *old woman.*

Madge. Welcome, Clunch, and good fellows all, that come
with my good man. For my good man's sake, come   60
on, sit down. Here is a piece of cheese and a pudding
of my own making.

Antic. Thanks, gammer; a good example for the wives of
our town.

Frolic. Gammer, thou and thy good man sit lovingly   65
together. We come to chat and not to eat.

Clunch. Well, masters, if you will eat nothing, take away.
Come, what do we to pass away the time? Lay a crab
in the fire to roast for lamb's-wool. What, shall we
have a game at trump or ruff to drive away the time?   70
How say you?

S.D. 55.1. *Here*] *Dyce; Heare Q.*   *barks*] *Dyce 1828; barke Q.*   S.D. 58.1.
MADGE, *an*] *Neilson.*   S.H. 59. *Madge.*] *Dyce 1861, passim; Ol. Q.*

54–5. *shall . . . be*] proverbial. See Tilley, T202, p. 661.

56–8.] The audience is to imagine a change of scene, or the scene shifts to one
of the various 'houses' on stage: here, Madge's cottage. See Intro., p. 30.

57–8. *stumbling on the threshold*] a bad luck sign.

68. *crab*] crabapple.

69. *lamb's-wool*] a drink made of hot ale mixed with the pulp of roasted apples,
and sugared and spiced.

70. *trump or ruff.*] The two names are sometimes used interchangeably for a
card game resembling whist, but at other times the two are distinguished. (See
O.E.D.)

Fantastic. This smith leads a life as merry as a king with
      Madge his wife. Sirrah Frolic, I am sure thou art not
      without some round or other. No doubt but Clunch
      can bear his part.   75
Frolic. Else think you me ill brought up. So set to it when
      you will.   *They sing.*

Song.

> *Whenas the rye reach to the chin,*
> *And chopcherry, chopcherry ripe within,*
> *Strawberries swimming in the cream,*   80
> *And schoolboys playing in the stream:*
> *Then O, then O, then O my true love said,*
> *Till that time come again,*
> *She could not live a maid.*

Antic. This sport does well. But, methinks, gammer, a   85
      merry winter's tale would drive away the time trimly.
      Come, I am sure you are not without a score.
Fantastic. I'faith, gammer, a tale of an hour long were as
      good as an hour's sleep.
Frolic. Look you, gammer, of the giant and the king's   90
      daughter, and I know not what. I have seen the day,
      when I was a little one, you might have drawn me a
      mile after you with such a discourse.
Madge. Well, since you be so importunate, my good man

78. *Whenas*] *(When as) Q.*

78–84.] Benjamin Britten composed a setting for the song in *Spring Symphony*.

79. chopcherry] a game in which people try to snatch with the mouth a cherry dangling from a string; also called 'bob cherry'.

86. *winter's tale*] The phrase traditionally connoted a light trifle 'not to be taken seriously' (see Pafford's introduction to *Wint.*, p. liii, n.3). Of course, part of the delight of both plays is that the audience is left with far more than a trifle. (See also *Mac.*, III.iv.63–5: 'O, these flaws and starts—/Imposters to true fear—would well become / A woman's story at a winter's fire'.)

88. *an hour long*] i.e. about the length of time the play itself takes on the stage; half or less than half the length of a normal Elizabethan play. Contrast 'two hours traffic of our stage' (*Rom.*, I. Chorus).

shall fill the pot and get him to bed. They that ply   95
their work must keep good hours. One of you go lie
with him. He is a clean skinned man I tell you,
without either spavin or windgall. So I am content to
drive away the time with an old wives winter's tale.

Fantastic. No better hay in Devonshire. A' my word,   100
gammer, I'll be one of your audience.

Frolic. And I another, that's flat.

Antic. Then must I to bed with the good man. *Bona nox*,
gammer. God night, Frolic.

Clunch. Come on, my lad; thou shalt take thy unnatural   105
rest with me.

Exeunt ANTIC *and* [CLUNCH] *the Smith.*

---

99. wives] *Q.;* wive's *Dyce 1828;* wives' *Dyce 1861.*   100. Devonshire.]
Baskervill; Devonshire, *Q.*   101. of] *Dyce;* of of *Q.*   104. God] *Q.;* Good
Dyce.

---

98. *spavin*] a tumour in a horse's leg, at the point where the splint-bone meets
the shank.

windgall] a tumour above a horse's fetlock. See *Shr.*, III.ii.53: 'full of wind-
galls, sped with spavins'.

99. *wives*] I retain Q. spelling, as any emendation is unsatisfactory. The
possessive singular *wife's* is, in fact, what is meant, making emendation to the
possessive plural *wives'* or to the fabrication *wive's* meaningless.

100. *hay in Devonshire*] way of spending the time. *Hay* = a country dance, of
the nature of a reel, as in 'rounds and winding Hays', Davies, *Orchestra*, stanza
lxiv, and 'dance an antic hay', Marlowe, *Edward II*, I.i.60. See J. S. Farmer and
W. E. Henley, *A Dictionary of Slang and Colloquial English* (abridged one vol.
ed., London, 1905, p. 217), to dance the hay = 'to make good use of one's time'.
There has been much speculation as to whether the phrase 'No better hay in
Devonshire' was proverbial, though it has not been encountered elsewhere; or
'if Peele's family were from Devon (see Horne, p. 10), he might have preserved
some local saying' (Hook, p. 424). Parts of Devonshire, particularly the South
Hams, happen to have some of the best agricultural land as well as warmest
climate in England for an excellent crop of hay; so the phrase came spontaneously. (Gen. ed.)

103. *Then must I to bed*] The actors playing Antic and Clunch likely doubled in
other rôles.

Bona nox] good night.

104. *God*] good. I follow Q., as it indicates the original meaning of the phrase:
'God give you good night.'

105–6. *unnatural rest*] Clunch's teasing joke, because the two men are sharing
the same bed.

Frolic. Yet this vantage shall we have of them in the morning, to be ready at the sight thereof extempore.

Madge. Now this bargain, my masters, must I make with you, that you will say hum and ha to my tale, so shall I know you are awake. 110

Both. Content, gammer; that will we do.

Madge. Once upon a time there was a king or a lord or a duke that had a fair daughter, the fairest that ever was; as white as snow and as red as blood; and once upon a time his daughter was stolen away, and he sent all his men to seek out his daughter, and he sent so long that he sent all his men out of his land. 115

Frolic. Who dressed his dinner, then?

Madge. Nay, either hear my tale, or kiss my tail. 120

Fantastic. Well said! On with your tale, gammer.

Madge. O Lord, I quite forgot! There was a conjurer, and this conjurer could do anything, and he turned himself into a great dragon, and carried the king's daughter away in his mouth to a castle that he made of stone, and there he kept her I know not how long; till at last all the king's men went out so long that her two brothers went to seek her. O, I forget! She (he, I would say) turned a proper young man to a bear in the night and a man in the day, and keeps by a cross that parts three several ways, and he made his lady 125

130

107–8.] The advantage Frolic and Fantastic will have over Clunch and Antic will be to see dawn break, if *extempore* is taken to mean 'at once, immediately' (*O.E.D.*).

113–15.] Madge's tale is crammed with folk motifs and the verbal formulas of old tales: 'once upon a time', 'white as snow', 'red as blood', etc. See Intro., pp. 21–3, for a discussion of Peele's folklore sources.

128. *two brothers*] Though the motif of the questing brothers is also found in *Comus*, there is no sure evidence that Peele's play was one of Milton's sources.

129. *proper*] handsome.

bear] The motifs of the 'helpful bear' and the transformation of man into bear occur frequently in folklore. See Intro., n. 59.

130. *keeps*] dwells. Crosses were commonly set up where roads met. Traditionally crossroads were places of magic power. See S. Thompson, *Motif-Index of Folk Literature* (Bloomington, Indiana, 1955) II, p. 318.

131. *he*] the conjurer.

run mad. Gods me bones! who comes here?

Enter the Two Brothers.

Frolic. Soft, gammer, here some come to tell your tale for
you.

Fantastic. Let them alone; let us hear what they will say.   135
First Brother. Upon these chalky cliffs of Albion
    We are arrivèd now with tedious toil,
    And compassing the wide world round about
    To seek our sister, to seek fair Delia forth,
    Yet cannot we so much as hear of her.   140
Second Brother. O Fortune cruel, cruel and unkind,
    Unkind in that we cannot find our sister,
    Our sister hapless in her cruel chance.
    Soft! who have we here?

Enter [ERESTUS] *Senex at the cross, stooping to gather.*

First Brother. Now father, God be your speed. What do   145
you gather there?
Erestus. Hips and haws, and sticks and straws, and things
that I gather on the ground, my son.
First Brother. Hips and haws, and sticks and straws. Why,
is that all your food, father?   150
Erestus. Yea, son.

139. to seek fair] *Q.*; seek fair *Bullen*; to seek *conj. Dyce 1861*.   S.D. 144.1.
ERESTUS] *Dyce 1861*.   S.H. 147. *Erestus.*] *Dyce 1861, passim; Old Man:
Q.*   147–8.] *as Q.*; hips . . . haws, / And . . . straws? / And . . . son. *Blair
subst.*   149–50.] *as Q.*; Hips . . . haws, / And . . . straws? / Why . . . father?
Blair subst.

---

136. *Upon these chalky cliffs . . .*] Gummere: 'The princes . . . talk in metre
when the "high style" is needed, but in familiar prose with Erestus.' Hook notes
(Intro., p. 304) that 'chalky cliffs' was a favourite phrase with Peele.
   139. *fair*] Probably the line should read as it stands, even though the scansion
is imperfect. Peele's metres are not always regular.
   144.1. ERESTUS] See *Dramatis Personae* n.
   147. *Hips and haws*] The hip is the fruit of the wild rose, the haw the fruit of
the hawthorn. The two words are used proverbially to indicate meagre fare, or
something of small worth. (The internal rhyme of this line is a recurring device
in prose passages in the play: e.g. 2, 161, 741–2, 748.)

Second Brother. Father, here is an alms-penny for me; and
   if I speed in that I go for, I will give thee as good a
   gown of grey as ever thou diddest wear.

First Brother. And, father, here is another alms-penny for   155
   me; and if I speed in my journey, I will give thee a
   palmer's staff of ivory and a scallop shell of beaten gold.

Erestus. Was she fair?

Second Brother. Ay, the fairest for white and the purest for
   red, as the blood of the deer or the driven snow.   160

Erestus. Then hark well, and mark well, my old spell:
   Be not afraid of every stranger,
   Start not aside at every danger;
   Things that seem are not the same,
   Blow a blast at every flame;   165
   For when one flame of fire goes out,
   Then comes your wishes well about.
   If any ask who told you this good,
   Say the White Bear of England's wood.

161.] *as Q.;* Then ... well, / And ... well, / My ... spell *Blair.*
167. comes] *Q.;* come *Dyce.*

---

152. *alms-penny*] the second gesture of spontaneous giving, the first being
Clunch's and Madge's hospitality.

   for me] for prayers for me.

154. *gown of grey*] together with the staff and the scallop shell (156), the
traditional garb and equipment of a palmer.

158. *Was she fair?*] The assumption by critics (e.g. Jenkins) that some lines
have dropped out of the text is not necessarily warranted. The audience requires
no explanation, and Erestus need not be told about Delia. See also Intro., pp.
13, 15 and 457 n.

162–9.] The lines are simple but have the elemental, gnomic power of
primitive riddling. The prophecy becomes relevant to other characters besides
the Brothers (e.g. Venelia will be the one who literally 'blows a blast' (875.1)).
The riddle concerns the total action of the play, as well as the moment at hand.
'Things that seem are not the same' lies at the heart of romantic metamorphosis
and discovery.

167. *comes*] a common form of the third person plural. See First Folio text of
Mer. V.: 'Where men inforced doth speak anything' (III.ii.33) and 'Hath all his
ventures faild?' (III.ii.269). See also 444, 544, 704, and 958 below.

169. *White Bear*] See Intro., p. 22 and n. 59.

First Brother. Brother, heard you not what the old man   170
    said?
    'Be not afraid of every stranger,
    Start not aside for every danger;
    Things that seem are not the same,
    Blow a blast at every flame;   175
    [For when one flame of fire goes out,
    Then comes your wishes well about.]
    If any ask who told you this good,
    Say the White Bear of England's wood.'
Second Brother. Well, if this do us any good,   180
    Well fare the White Bear of England's wood.
                      Ex[eunt the Two Brothers].
Erestus. Now sit thee here and tell a heavy tale,
    Sad in thy mood and sober in thy cheer.
    Here sit thee now and to thyself relate
    The hard mishap of thy most wretched state.   185
    In Thessaly I lived in sweet content,
    Until that Fortune wrought my overthrow.
    For there I wedded was unto a dame
    That lived in honour, virtue, love, and fame.
    But Sacrapant, that cursèd sorcerer,   190
    Being besotted with my beauteous love,
    My dearest love, my true betrothèd wife,
    Did seek the means to rid me of my life.
    But worse than this, he with his chanting spells
    Did turn me straight unto an ugly bear;   195

172–79. 'Be . . . wood'] *quotation marks by Neilson.*   176–7.] *as Dyce 1861*
subst.   S.D. 181.1.] *as Dyce; ex. Q.*

---

183. *cheer*] countenance.

186. *Thessaly*] 'the birthplace of sorceries and enchantments' (Apuleius, p. 49). See Intro., p. 20.

188. *wedded*] Though it is possible for the riddle of a lady being 'neither wife, widow, nor maid' (449) to be solved (as in *Measure for Measure*, where Claudio and Juliet are legally married, but their union has not been consecrated by the Church), pondering resolutions is not appropriate here. Irreconcilables are expected, and the viewers are not meant to become Duke Vincentios.

190. *Sacrapant*] See *Dramatis Personae* n.

194. *chanting*] aphetic form of 'enchanting'.

And when the sun doth settle in the west,
Then I begin to don my ugly hide.
And all the day I sit, as now you see,
And speak in riddles, all inspired with rage,
Seeming an old and miserable man,   200
And yet I am in April of my age.

Enter VENELIA *his lady, mad; and goes in again.*

See where Venelia, my betrothèd love,
Runs madding all enraged about the woods,
All by his cursèd and enchanting spells.

Enter LAMPRISCUS *with a pot of honey.*

But here comes Lampriscus, my discontented neigh-   205
bour. How now, neighbour; you look toward the
ground as well as I. You muse on something.
Lampriscus. Neighbour, on nothing, but on the matter I so
often moved to you. If you do anything for charity,
help me; if for neighbourhood or brotherhood, help   210

S.D. 204.1] *as Q.; after* neighbour, 205–6, *Dyce 1861*.

199. *rage*] prophetic inspiration or 'fury'.
201. *April of my age*] Though the phrase is a commonplace (see *The Rare Triumphs of Love and Fortune (Malone Society Reprints*, line 583)), its effect in *Old Wives Tale* is stronger than that of bland cliché. The phrase is first spoken by a seeming old man, then, in a parody situation, by the braggart Huanebango (698). When Eumenides, a man really in the April of his age, speaks the line (721), it carries authentic poignancy.
201.1.] As with 875.1–3, the action takes more time than a mere reading of the stage directions indicates. The effect can be magical rather than comic.
207. *ground*] Note that much of the action and stage business of the play has to do more with an 'earth spirit' than with those of other elements—in keeping with the basic earthiness of original folk tales. Lampriscus and Erestus are linked in misfortune, and here both 'look toward the ground'. The Two Brothers, wandering on the earth, are lost in the dark woods; Sacrapant punishes the Brothers by having them dig in the soil; he himself has buried his magic light; the two Heads, and Huanebango, rise in the well, from under the earth; the action concerning Eumenides and Jack begins with the ceremonies of burial; at the play's conclusion Jack 'leaps down in the ground' (950.1).
209. *for charity*] The thematic centre of the play comes to the fore once more. In 211 Lampriscus gives, even though he himself has just asked for help.

me; never was one so cumbered as is poor Lampriscus. And to begin, I pray receive this pot of honey
to mend your fare.

Erestus. Thanks, neighbour; set it down.

[*Aside*] Honey is always welcome to the bear.—   215
And now, neighbour, let me hear the cause of your
coming.

Lampriscus. I am (as you know, neighbour) a man unmar-
ried, and lived so unquietly with my two wives, that I
keep every year holy the day wherein I buried them   220
both. The first was on Saint Andrew's day, the other
on Saint Luke's.

Erestus. And now, neighbour, you of this country say:
your custom is out. But on with your tale, neighbour.

Lampriscus. By my first wife, whose tongue wearied me   225
alive, and sounded in my ears like the clapper of a
great bell, whose talk was a continual torment to all
that dwelt by her, or lived nigh her, you have heard
me say I had a handsome daughter.

Erestus. True, neighbour.   230

215.] *as Q.; prose in Dyce.*

---

211. *cumbered*] harassed, troubled, as in St Luke x.40: 'Martha was cumbered about much serving'.

215.] I follow Q. in printing this as a verse line, for doing so seems to retain the
line's gnomic flavour. See Tilley, B130, H551. Lampriscus' gift is the fourth
gesture of charity.

221–2. *Saint Andrew's . . . Saint Luke's*] Folk celebrations on these saints'
days were survivals of fertility rituals. On both days, lovers could get their
hearts' desires. Lampriscus' good luck is that he gets rid of his wives. His
daughters later (637, 644) express wishes like those in lovers' prayers traditionally said on St Andrew's day (30 Nov.) and on St Luke's (18 Oct.); '*Deus, Deus
meus, O Sancte Andrea effice et bonum pium acquiram viram; hodie mihi ostende
qualis fit cui me in uxorem ducere debat*' (Brand, *Popular Antiquities*, ed. Hazlitt, I,
p. 228); 'St Luke, St Luke be kind to me,/In dreams let me my love see' (Wright
& Lones, *British Calendar Customs*, III, p. 100).

224. *custom*] obligatory service, due by feudal tenants to their lord. Erestus is
implying that Lampriscus was mastered by these women, but that now he is
free. Out = over.

Lampriscus. She it is that afflicts me with her continual
    clamours and hangs on me like a bur. Poor she is, and
    proud she is—as poor as a sheep new-shorn and as
    proud of her hopes as a peacock of her tail well-grown.
Erestus. Well said, Lampriscus. You speak it like an   235
    Englishman.
Lampriscus. As curst as a wasp, and as froward as a child
    new-taken from the mother's teat. She is to my age as
    smoke to the eyes or as vinegar to the teeth.
Erestus. Holily praised, neighbour. As much for the next.   240
Lampriscus. By my other wife I had a daughter so hard-
    favoured, so foul and ill-faced, that I think a grove
    full of golden trees, and the leaves of rubies and
    diamonds, would not be a dowry answerable to her
    deformity.   245
Erestus. Well, neighbour, now you have spoke, hear me
    speak. Send them to the well for the water of life.
    There shall they find their fortunes unlooked for.
    Neighbour, farewell.   [*Withdraws.*]

S.D. 249. *Withdraws*] *This ed.; Hook conj.; Exit Q.*

232–3. *Poor . . . proud*] The two words are often combined proverbially
(Tilley, P474). Here, and below (231–9), Lampriscus' speeches are full of
proverbs. See Tilley, under 'sheep', 'peacock', 'wasp', 'vinegar'. Lampriscus'
earthy realism and natural vigour of expression are admired by Erestus: 'You
speak it like an Englishman' (235–6).

   237. *curst*] shrewish.

   froward] refractory.

   240. *Holily praised*] Hook notes that Lampriscus has been quoting scripture:
'As vinegar to the teeth, and as smoke to the eyes, so is the sluggard to them that
send him' (Proverbs, x.26).

   242. *foul*] ugly.

   247. *well . . . water of life*] common folklore, and biblical, motifs. See Intro.,
pp. 21–2.

   249. S.D.] Erestus probably withdraws, rather than actually leaving the
stage. When Corebus and Huanebango later encounter him (316), an entrance is
not marked in Q. In some ways he can be seen as the presiding prophetic spirit of
the play. Like Madge, the other 'presider', he need never leave the stage, though
he can at times withdraw.

Lampriscus. Farewell and a thousand! And now goeth   250
  poor Lampriscus to put in execution this excellent
  counsel.   *Exit.*
Frolic. Why, this goes round without a fiddling stick. But
  do you hear, gammer? was this the man that was a
  bear in the night and a man in the day?   255
Madge. Ay, this is he; and this man that came to him was a
  beggar and dwelt upon a green. But soft, who comes
  here? O, these are the harvest-men; ten to one they
  sing a song of mowing.

Enter the Harvest-men *a-singing, with this song double-repeated.*

> All ye that lovely lovers be,   260
> Pray you for me.
> Lo, here we come a-sowing, a-sowing,

S.D. 252. *Exit*] Dyce; *Exeunt Q.*   257. comes] *Q.;* come *Dyce 1861.*
260–1. *All . . . be, | Pray . . . me.*] *Dyce 1861; one line in Q.*

---

250. *Farewell and a thousand*] a thousand times farewell, as in Middleton's *A Trick to Catch the Old One*: 'let me hug thee; farewell and a thousand' (*Works*, ed. Dyce, II, p. 86).

253. *round . . . stick*] See 100 n. Madge's tale is as fast and entertains as well as a country dance to a fiddler's tune. The phrase may have been proverbial, as Hook suggests.

257. *beggar . . . green*] traditional phrase, from ballads and folklore. See 'The Beggar's Daughter of Bednall Green' (Percy, *Reliques*, (1767) II, p. 155) and Day and Chettle's play *The Blind Beggar of Bednall Green* (1600).

259.1. *Harvest-men*] The unmotivated appearance of the Harvest-men, and the break in sequential plot, is not the result of slipshod construction, but is common to dramatic romance and to masques and entertainments.

262. *a-sowing*] Madge's wager (258–9) is logical, but the harvesters sing of sowing. This is not a slip for 'mowing'; the conflation of times is traditional in folk play and dramatic romance. In the marriage masque in *Tp.* Ceres asks that 'Spring come to you at the farthest, / In the very end of harvest' (IV.i.114–15). In *Wint.* Autolycus sings a spring song in summer (IV.iii.1 ff.). Time conflation is implied throughout the scenes of pastoral festivity in *Wint.* Sheep-shearing usually occurs in late June (Drayton, 'Ninth Eclogue' (*Works*, ed. Hebel, II, p. 564)), but Perdita distributes flowers of late summer. T. F. Ordish's 'English Folk-Drama' (*Folk-Lore*, IV, p. 169) notes that 'the joining of motifs from various portions of the agricultural year was apparently customary in folk festivals.'

And sow sweet fruits of love.
In your sweet hearts well may it prove.   *Exeunt.*

Enter HUANEBANGO *with his two-hand sword, and*
COREBUS *the Clown.*

Fantastic. Gammer, what is he?   265
Madge. O, this is one that is going to the conjurer. Let him
    alone; hear what he says.
Huanebango. Now, by Mars and Mercury, Jupiter and
    Janus, Sol and Saturnus, Venus and Vesta, Pallas and
    Proserpina, and by the honour of my house Polimac-   270
    keroplacidus, it is a wonder to see what this love will
    make silly fellows adventure, even in the wane of
    their wits and infancy of their discretion. Alas, my
    friend, what fortune calls thee forth to seek thy for-
    tune among brazen gates, enchanted towers, fire and   275

S.D. 264.2. COREBUS] *Dyce 1861;* Booby *Q.*

264.1.HUANEBANGO] See *Dramatis Personae* n.
    two-hand sword] Cheffaud, p. 124, and Blair find here an allusion to Harvey
and his boasts about fencing. Nashe uses the term when describing Harvey: 'An
olde Fencer . . . flourishing about my eares with his two hand swords of Oratory
and Poetry' (I, p. 262). But Huanebango and his sword seem more closely
connected to folk drama and mumming. See the accounts of Midsummer Shows
in Malone Society *Collections*, III, pp. 16, 17, 22, for indication of the popularity
of the figures of giants and performers with two-hand swords.
    264.2.COREBUS] See *Dramatis Personae* n.
    268–70. *Mars . . . Proserpina*] Huanebango swears by practically the whole
cosmos but, as in all his grandiose language, the sound of the words is more
important than their meanings.
    270–1. *Polimackeroeplacidus*] In an attempt to see Huanebango as a satiric
portrait of Gabriel Harvey, Fleay deciphered this name 'Poly-make-a-rope-lass',
an aspersion on the trade of Harvey's father, ropemaker (*Biog. Chronicle*, II, p.
155). Gummere comments, 'Mr. Fleay is bold.' Peele is simply imitating
Plautus' long, mouth-filling names:
    Bellio.   *Oh, Polymachaeroplagides,*
        purus putus est ipsus. novi. heus, Polymachaeroplagides
        nomen est.
                                            (*Pseudolus,* 988–90)
    274–83. *seek thy fortune . . . kill conjuring*] the archetypal perils and labours of
the quester. As usual, Huanebango speaks 'more in word than matter'. Note
that other characters do in reality what Huanebango brags about in 281–3.

brimstone, thunder and lightning? Beauty, I tell
thee, is peerless, and she precious whom thou affect-
est. Do off these desires, good countryman; good
friend, run away from thyself, and so soon as thou
canst, forget her, whom none must inherit but he that   280
can monsters tame, labours achieve, riddles absolve,
loose enchantments, murder magic, and kill conjuring: and that is the great and mighty Huanebango.

Corebus. Hark you, sir, hark you. First know I have here
the flurting feather, and have given the parish the   285
start for the long stock. Now, sir, if it be no more but
running through a little lightning and thunder, and
'riddle me, riddle me, what's this?' I'll have the

---

276. Beauty] *Q.*; Her beauty *conj. Dyce 1861.*   S.H. 284. *Corebus.*]*Dyce
1861, passim to 351; Booby Q.*   288. 'riddle . . . this?'] *quotation marks by
Dyce 1861.*

---

276. *Beauty*] Emendation to 'Her beauty' is unnecessary. As far as
Huanebango's bombast can be expected to make sense, the line seems to mean:
'There is nothing that can compare with beauty, and she whom you love is the
most precious beauty of all.'

278. *Do off*] doff.

278-9. *countryman . . . friend*] Huanebango means himself, rather than
Corebus. He begins by addressing himself (273), then counsels himself, and
ends by praising himself. The 'thou' is always himself, and he never moves from
this favourite subject.

285. *flurting*] moving with a whisking, jaunty motion.

285-6. *given . . . the start . . . stock*] a troublesome line. Dyce took 'stock' to
mean 'sword' and commented, 'Corebus means . . . that he has run away from
the parish and become a . . . knight errant.' Bullen agreed neither with Dyce
nor Dr Brinsley Nicholson (who interpreted the line to mean that Corebus had
fled from the parish to avoid being put in the stocks) and commented, 'The
Clown is pluming himself on his finery . . . [his] feather and . . . fashionable
long stock, i.e. the stocking fastened high above the knee.' Gummere, Neilson,
Blair, and Hook follow Bullen's interpretation. Gummere adds, 'Corebus
asserts a sort of equality with Huanebango.' Hook conjectures that Corebus apes
Huanebango's finery (traditional for braggart soldiers), but that Corebus'
clothes actually are outmoded: 'As Huanebango is a parody of the Knight
Errant, so the Clown is a parody of Huanebango.' '[Give] the start' would, in this
context, mean 'to astonish'; the line may be paraphrased 'I have startled the
parish with my fine long stocking.'

288. *riddle me*]The riddling tradition is as ancient as the folklore in the play.
Riddles are themselves an essential motif in folklore and legend. For a discussion of the ritual origins of riddle see J. Huizinga, *Homo Ludens*, pp. 105–18.

wench from the conjurer, if he were ten conjurers.

Huanebango. I have abandoned the court and honourable   290
  company, to do my devoir against this sore sorcerer
  and mighty magician. If this lady be so fair as she is
  said to be, she is mine, she is mine. *Meus, mea, meum,*
  in contemptum omnium grammaticorum.

Corebus. O falsum Latinum!   295
  The fair maid is *minum,*
  Cum apurtinantibus gibletes and all.

Huanebango. If she be mine (as I assure myself the heavens
  will do somewhat to reward my worthiness) she shall
  be allied to none of the meanest gods, but be invested   300
  in the most famous stock of Huanebango Polimack-
  eroeplacidus, my grandfather; my father, Pergopolineo; my mother, Dionara de Sardinia, fam-
  ously descended.

Corebus. Do you hear, sir? Had not you a cousin that was   305
  called Gusteceridis?

Huanebango. Indeed, I had a cousin that sometime followed the court infortunately, and his name Bus-
  tegusteceridis.

295–7.] *as Dyce 1861; prose in Q.*   297. *gibletes*] *Q.; gibletis Dyce 1861.*

---

291. *devoir*] duty (in chivalric parlance).

sore] causing trouble, distress.

293–4. Meus . . . grammaticorum] By claiming the lady in three genders,
Huanebango omits no possibility of possessing her, at least in pedantic fantasy.
Blair notes that 'she' was played by a boy; and that as long as Huanebango has
taken this into account by using two genders, he might as well go the whole way
and use all three.

297. cum apurtinantibus] a legal term: 'with its appurtenances'.

gibletes] nonsense Latin; Corebus means giblets.

302–3. *Pergopolineo*] Here (as in 270 and 301–2, above; and 306, 308–9,
below) Peele imitates Plautine names (Pergopolynices, in *Miles Gloriosus*). Fleay
translated Pergopolineo 'Perg-up-a-line-o', to equate Huanebango's father with
Harvey's ropemaker parent; but it seems clear that Huanebango's ancestry is
closer to that of the Plautine braggart soldier than it is to Harvey's.

303. *Dionara de Sardinia*] unidentifiable. Perhaps it is Peele's invention?

Corebus. O Lord, I know him well! He is the Knight of the   310
    Neat's Feet.

Huanebango. O, he loved no capon better. He hath often-
    times deceived his boy of his dinner. That was his
    fault, good Bustegusteceridus.

Corebus. Come, shall we go along?   315

[ERESTUS *comes forward.*]

Soft! here is an old man at the cross. Let us ask him
    the way thither. Ho, you gaffer! I pray you tell where
    the wise man the conjurer dwells.

Huanebango. Where that earthly goddess keepeth her
    abode, the commander of my thoughts, and fair mis-   320
    tress of my heart.

Erestus. Fair enough, and far enough from thy fingering,
    son.

Huanebango. I will follow my fortune after mine own
    fancy, and do according to mine own discretion.   325

Erestus. Yet give something to an old man before you go.

Huanebango. Father, methinks a piece of this cake might
    serve your turn.

Erestus. Yea, son.

Huanebango. Huanebango giveth no cakes for alms. Ask   330
    of them that give gifts for poor beggars. Fair lady, if

S.D. 315.1] *This ed.; Enter* ERESTUS *Dyce (after* cross, *316); not in Q.*   S.H.
327. *Huanebango.*] (*Huau:*) *Q.; Booby conj. Blair.*   330. Huanebango]
(Huanabango) *Q.*

---

311. *Neat's Feet*] feet of an ox (or bullock, cow, etc. (*O.E.D.*)). Huanebango
may be proud of his pedigree, but the heraldic device actually makes his lineage
look ridiculous. Oxen's or cows' feet were the scraps used to make brawn (see
Dorothy Hartland, *Food in England*, London, 1954, p. 80). A loose paraphrase
conveying the meaning of the device could be 'Knight of the Leftovers' or
'Knight of the Stock Pot'.

313. *deceived*] used with 'of' to mean 'cheat out of'.

315.1. S.D.] See 249 n.

327–8. Blair conjectures that the lines may be Corebus', but there is no
difficulty in having Huanebango say them. He speaks in a teasing mood.

thou wert once shrined in this bosom, I would buckler thee! Haratantara!   *Exit.*

Corebus. Father, do you see this man? You little think
he'll run a mile or two for such a cake, or pass for a   335
pudding. I tell you, father, he has kept such a begging
of me for a piece of this cake. Whoo! He comes upon
me with a 'superfantial substance, and the foison of
the earth,' that I know not what he means. If he came
to me thus and said 'My friend Corebus,' or so, why I   340
could spare him a piece with all my heart; but when
he tells me how God hath enriched me above other
fellows with a cake; why, he makes me blind and deaf
at once. Yet father, here is a piece of cake for you, as
hard as the world goes.   345

Erestus. Thanks, son, but list to me:
He shall be deaf when thou shalt not see.
Farewell, my son; things may so hit,
Thou mayst have wealth to mend thy wit.

Corebus. Farewell, father farewell; for I must make haste   350

---

333. thee! Haratantara!] *This ed.;* thee haratantara. *Q., Dyce.*   38–9. a
'superfantial . . . earth,'] *McIlwraith;* a superfantial . . . earth, *Q.;* 'a superfantial . . . earth,' *Dyce 1861.*   340. 'My . . . Corebus,'] *quotation marks by Dyce
1861.*   340. Corebus] *Dyce 1861; Booby Q.*   344. you,] *Dyce;* you *Q.*

332–3. *buckler*] shield.
335. *pass for*] care for. *O.E.D.* quotes Ascham (*Schoolmaster*, 1568, ed. Arber,
I, p. 82): 'They passe for no Doctores: They mocke the Pope: They raile on
Luther.'
338–9. *superfantial . . . earth*] Corebus' imitation of Huanebango's bombast.
On the meaning of 'superfantial' McIlwraith comments, 'The *O.E.D.* shares
Corebus' ignorance of this word.'
344. *cake*] another example of the gift freely given. See Intro., p. 22 for
folklore parallels.
344–5. *as hard as the world goes*] The phrase means 'though times are hard',
not that Corebus' cake is. Inserting a comma after 'you' helps to convey this
sense. Dyce and Hook refer to *2 Return from Parnassus*: 'Ile moyst thy temples
with a cuppe of Claret, as hard as the world goes' (I.ii.334, ed. Leishman,
London, 1949).

after my two-hand sword that is gone before.

Exeunt omnes.

Enter SACRAPANT *in his study.*

Sacrapant. The day is clear, the welkin bright and grey;
    The lark is merry and records her notes;
    Each thing rejoiceth underneath the sky,
    But only I, whom heaven hath in hate: 355
    Wretched and miserable Sacrapant.
    In Thessaly was I born and brought up;
    My mother Meroe hight, a famous witch,
    And by her cunning I of her did learn
    To change and alter shapes of mortal men.   360
    There did I turn myself into a dragon,
    And stole away the daughter to the king,
    Fair Delia, the mistress of my heart;
    And brought her hither to revive the man
    That seemeth young and pleasant to behold,   365
    And yet is agèd, crooked, weak and numb.
    Thus by enchanting spells I do deceive

---

352. grey] (gray) *Q.;* gay *Blair.*

351.1. Exeunt omnes] Madge, Frolic and Fantastic are still on stage. In Greg's
'new vampt' version, Corebus is played by Fantastic, and he would at this point
re-enter the dimension of Madge's world. Greg does not claim that *OWT* was
performed with the parts doubled in the manner he suggests, but his idea is
intriguing. His method of staging would make more intricate the relation of
levels of reality and illusion.

351.2. study] An 'inner stage', or some kind of alcove with curtains before it,
was commonly used as a conjurer's 'study' or cell (*cf.* 657.1 below). See *Friar
Bacon and Friar Bungay* (ed. D. Seltzer, Regents Renaissance Drama), scenes
vi, xi; and *Dr. Faustus* (ed. J. D. Jump, Revels Plays), scenes i, v, vi, xviii.

352. *grey*] blue, as in Chaucer, *Knight's Tale*, 1491–4:
            The bisy larke, messager of day,
            Salueth in hir song the morwe gray,
            And firy Phebus riseth up so bright
            That al the orient laugheth of the light. (So Hook.)

353. *records*] sings.

357. *Thessaly*] See 186 n.

358. *Meroe*] The Thessalonian witch who enchanted Socrates (Apuleius, p.
13).

Those that behold and look upon my face;
But well may I bid youthful years adieu.

Enter DELIA *with a pot in her hand.*

See where she comes, from whence my sorrows grow. 370
How now, fair Delia, where have you been?

Delia. At the foot of the rock for running water, and
gathering roots for your dinner, sir.

Sacrapant. Ah Delia, fairer art thou than the running
water, yet harder far than steel or adamant. 375

Delia. Will it please you to sit down, sir?

Sacrapant. Ay, Delia, sit and ask me what thou wilt. Thou
shalt have it brought into thy lap.

Delia. Then I pray you, sir, let me have the best meat
from the king of England's table, and the best wine in 380
all France, brought in by the veriest knave in all
Spain.

Sacrapant. Delia, I am glad to see you so pleasant. Well, sit
thee down:

Spread, table, spread, 385
Meat, drink and bread.
Ever may I have
What I ever crave.
When I am spread,

---

370. comes,] *Dyce 1828;* coms *Q.* 374–5.] *as Q.;* Ah, Delia, / Fairer . . .
water, / Yet . . . adamant! *Dyce.* 377–8.] *as Q.;* Ay . . . wilt, / Thou . . . lap
Dyce. 383–4.] *as Q.;* Delia . . . pleasant:/Well . . . down *Dyce.* 385.
Spread] *Dyce; Sacr:* Spred *Q.* 385–6.] *as Dyce; one line in Q.* 387–8.] *as
Dyce; one line in Q.* 389–90.] *as Dyce; one line in Q.*

372–84.] Though lines that can be read as iambic pentameter appear in this
passage: e.g. 'yet harder far than steel or adamant' a375), 'Ay, Delia, sit and ask
me what thou wilt. / Thou shalt have it brought into thy lap' (377–8), I prefer to
follow Q., it being unlikely that a few verse lines would occur, unless for a
specific purpose, in a passage which is otherwise prose.

For meat for my black cock,   390
And meat for my red.

Enter a Friar *with a chine of beef and a pot of wine.*

Sacrapant. Here, Delia; will ye fall to?
Delia. Is this the best meat in England?
Sacrapant. Yea.
Delia. What is it?   395
Sacrapant. A chine of English beef—meat for a king and a
      king's followers.
Delia. Is this the best wine in France?
Sacrapant. Yea.
Delia. What wine is it?   400
Sacrapant. A cup of neat wine of Orleans, that never came
      near the brewers in England.
Delia. Is this the veriest knave in all Spain?
Sacrapant. Yea.

390. For meat] *Q. subst.;* Meat *Dyce 1861.*   396–7.] *as Dyce;* A . . . king /
And . . . followers *Q.*   401–2.] *as Dyce;* A . . . *Orleance,* / That . . . England
Q.

---

390. *For meat*] I retain Q., but Dyce's emendation, to make the metre regular,
may be justified.

390–1. *black cock . . . red*] Cocks are traditionally associated with the supernatural, with magic and divination, and their colours are important. Gummere
refers to 'The Wife of Usher's Well', in which the Wife is visited by the ghosts of
her drowned sons:

> Up then crew the red, red cock,
> And up and crew the gray;
> The eldest to the youngest said,
> ''Tis time we were away.'
>   (*English Verse*, ed. W. Peacock, II, p. 495)

391.1. *chine*] backbone, and surrounding flesh—which, for beef, would be
ribs or sirloin.

396. *and*] Q. begins a new line here (and also at 401: 'That never came . . .'),
but both speeches are clearly prose. As Blair suggests, the printer had probably
'in setting up the . . . verse gotten into the habit of capitalizing new lines'.

401. *neat*] not mixed with water, undiluted.

402. *brewers in England*] commonly marred 'their malt with water' (*Lr.*,
III.ii.82). To 'brew' also means to mix liquor with water.

403. *knave*] In anti-Catholic propaganda, especially in the time of antagonism
to Spain, friars were railed against.

Delia. What is he? a friar? 405

Sacrapant. Yea, a friar indefinite, and a knave infinite.

Delia. Then I pray ye, Sir Friar, tell me before you go,
    which is the most greediest Englishman?

Friar. The miserable and most covetous usurer.

Sacrapant. Hold thee there, friar! *Exit* Friar. 410
    But soft, who have we here? Delia, away, begone!

Enter the Two Brothers.

Delia, away! for beset are we,
But heaven or hell shall rescue her for me.

[*Exeunt* SACRAPANT *and* DELIA.]

First Brother. Brother, was not that Delia did appear?
    Or was it but her shadow that was here? 415

Second Brother. Sister, where art thou? Delia, come again.
    He calls, that of thy absence doth complain.

---

405. What is he?] *This ed.;* What is he *Q.;* What, is he *Dyce;* What is he,
McIlwraith.   410–11.] *as Q.;* Hold . . . soft! / Who . . . be gone! *Dyce*
1861.   413. or] *Q.;* nor *Bullen.*   for] *Q.;* from *conj. Bullen.*   S.D.
413.1.] *Dyce.*

405.] Q.'s lack of punctuation permits the line to be read in two ways: 'What is
he, a friar?' (or 'What is he? a friar?') and 'What, is he a friar?' (or 'What? is he a
friar?'). The first of the two possible readings conveys the impression that Delia
does not know the answer to the question—which seems more likely.

406. *friar indefinite*] uncertain meaning. Hook suggests, 'If there is anything
more here than a play with words, it may be the opposite of a "friar limiter", a
friar licensed to beg in a restricted area, like Chaucer's "Lymytour".'

409. *usurer*] See Intro., p. 15.

410. *Hold thee there*] Hold fast to that opinion. See Intro., pp. 13, 15–16.

413.] The line makes sense as it stands, though most editors have either
emended it or found it difficult. Sacrapant is saying, 'We are beset, but
heaven—or hell—shall keep her safe for me.'

413.1.] It is obvious that Delia exits here (perhaps to Sacrapant's cell). It
appears that Sacrapant exits also, and does not re-enter until 435.1. However,
David Blostein's production (Toronto, 1969) handled the subsequent 'echo'
episode (420 ff.) in an interesting way. Sacrapant did not actually exit after 413,
but remained to play the part of the echo, lurking in the woods, 'invisible',
luring the Brothers closer.

415. *shadow*] The debate between shadow and substance, appearance and
reality, is essential to the play.

Call out, Calypha, that she may hear,
And cry aloud, for Delia is near.
Echo. Near.   420
First Brother. Near! O where? Hast thou any tidings?
Echo. Tidings.
Second Brother. Which way is Delia then? or that, or this?
Echo. This.
First Brother. And may we safely come where Delia is?   425
Echo. Yes.
Second Brother. Brother, remember you the White Bear of
        England's wood:
    'Start not aside for every danger,
    Be not afeard of every stranger;   430
    Things that seem are not the same.'
First Brother. Brother, why do we not then courageously
        enter?
Second Brother. Then, brother, draw thy sword and follow
        me.   435

        Enter [SACRAPANT] *the Conjurer. It lightens and thun-
            ders. The* Second Brother *falls down.*

418. that] *Q.;* call that *conj. Dyce 1861.*   421. Near!] *Dyce;* Neere, *Q.;* Neere?
Gummere.   423. then?[*Dyce 1861;* then, *Q.*   429–31.] *quotation marks by
Dyce 1861.*

---

418. *Calypha*] The First Brother has not been identified previously, but this
poses no problem. That Sacrapant automatically knows his name (437) does not
necessarily indicate that an earlier part of the action has dropped out. Magicians
always know these things. I cannot trace the origin of the name.

420. Echo] The voice of an echo giving aid or answers to the speaker became a
dramatic convention. See Webster's *Duchess of Malfi,* V. iii (*c.* 1614); Jonson's
Masque of Blackness (1605) and *Masque of Beauty* (1608), vol. VII, pp. 179 and
190; and Dekker's *Old Fortunatus,* I.i. Examples previous to *OWT* are less
readily found. Peele himself uses the device in *The Arraignment of Paris,* 1594
(Yale Peele, III, p. 70). See also Lyly's Entertainment at Elvetham, 1591: 'and
the end of every verse was replied by Lutes and voices in the other boate
somwhat a farre off, as if they had beene Ecchoes' (*Works,* ed. R. W. Bond, I,
pp. 443–4). Guy Hamel, University of Toronto, suggested a possible background for the tradition: Erasmus' 'Echo' colloquy, 1526.

423. *or that, or this?*] this way, or that way?

435.1. Enter] Sacrapant may not actually have exited. See 413.1 n.

First Brother. What, brother, dost thou fall?
Sacrapant. Ay, and thou too, Calypha.

      Fall First Brother. *Enter* Two Furies.

Adeste Daemones! Away with them!
Go carry them straight to Sacrapanto's cell,
There in despair and torture for to dwell.   440
      [*Exeunt* Furies *with the* Two Brothers.]
These are Thenore's sons of Thessaly,
That come to seek Delia their sister forth;
But with a potion I to her have given,
My arts hath made her to forget herself.

   He removes a turf, and shows a light in a glass.

See here the thing which doth prolong my life.   445
With this enchantment I do anything;
And till this fade, my skill shall still endure.
And never none shall break this little glass
But she that's neither wife, widow, nor maid.

S.D. 437.1. *Enter* Two Furies] *as Q.; after Daemones*, 438, *Dyce 1861; and carry them off, added by Hook.*   438. *Adeste*] *Dyce 1861; Adestes Q.*   S.D. 440.1.] *Dyce.*   444. hath] *Q.;* have *Dyce.*

440.1.] I follow Dyce in having the Furies exit here. (Hook combines their entrance and exit in a single stage direction at 437.1.) Sacrapant's speech (441–51) sounds like a soliloquy rather than an address to the Brothers and the Furies. I therefore emend Q.'s *Exeunt* (451) to *Exit.*

441. *Thenore's sons*] The Brothers have introduced themselves earlier (135), but the repetition should not bother the audience. As Hook comments, 'redundancy is the rule of the play' (p. 346). It is also the rule of fairy tales. I cannot trace the origin of the name Thenore.

443. *potion*] The motif of the potion likewise appears in *Comus*. Delia, like the Lady, is subsequently immobilised through the enchanter's art (880.1). But, again, these similarities do not prove that Milton's source was Peele.

444. *arts hath*] See 167n.

444.1.] The phrasing of the stage directions seems to indicate the author's hand. See Intro., p. 11. The motif of the 'life-index' is common in folklore. See J. G. Frazer, *The Golden Bough*, IX, pp. 160 ff.

449.] The riddle of the woman who was 'neither wife, widow, nor maid' was well known. See *Meas.*, V.i.171–80.

Then cheer thyself; this is thy destiny: 450
Never to die, but by a dead man's hand.   *Exit.*

Enter EUMENIDES *the Wandering Knight.*

Eumenides. Tell me, Time; tell me, just Time,
      When shall I Delia see?
      When shall I see the lodestar of my life?
      When shall my wandering course end with her sight,   455
      Or I but view my hope, my heart's delight?

Enter [ERESTUS] *the Old Man at the cross.*

Father, God speed! If you tell fortunes, I pray, good
father, tell me mine.

Erestus. Son, I do see in thy face
      Thy blessèd fortune work apace.   460
      I do perceive that thou hast wit;
      Beg of thy fate to govern it,

---

451. die,] *Q.; die Dyce.*   S.D. *Exit*] *Dyce; Exeunt Q.*   S.D.'s 451.1 and
456.1 *Enter* . . . *Knight.* . . . *Enter* . . . *cross.*] *Dyce 1861; Enter* Eumenides *the
wandring Knight, and the old man at the crosse. Q. (after line 451).*   452–3.] *as
Q.;* Tell . . . Time, / Tell . . . see *Dyce.*   455. sight,] *Dyce,* sight? *Q.*

---

451. *die,*] If Q.'s comma is omitted, the sentence becomes less emphatic.
Retaining the comma gives force to the first clause: '*Never to die* (but by a dead
man's hand).' Sacrapant's belief in his immortality is conveyed more surely in
Q.

452–3.] I retain Q.'s lineation, though the metre is irregular. The effect of the
accumulation of lines beginning with 'when' seems more vital than regular
rhythm. Line 452 flows well, with its repeated phrase.

454. *lodestar of my life*] The phrase (or ones similar to it) was a commonplace.
For the Peele canon, Hook refers one to *Edward I*, 938; *Alcazar*, 104; *Honour of
the Garter*, 392.

456.1. Enter ERESTUS] Erestus does not approach until this point, though Q.
has him enter at 451.1. See also 249 n. It is of course possible that Erestus enters
from another door (or from his 'station') at 451, but is seen by Eumenides only at
457.

457. *If you tell fortunes*] That Eumenides surmises Erestus' function shows
again how the play follows the narrative methods of fairy tale, where logical
preparation and sequence are not needed.

461. *wit*] mental gifts.

462. *Beg . . .it*] i.e. Pray that your wit may develop into wisdom. But one
should beware of interpreting lines of riddling verse too literally.

For wisdom governed by advice
Makes many fortunate and wise.
Bestow thy alms, give more than all,   465
Till dead men's bones come at thy call.
Farewell, my son; dream of no rest,
Till thou repent that thou didst best. *Exit* [ERESTUS].
Eumenides. This man hath left me in a labyrinth.
He biddeth me give more than all,   470
'Till dead men's bones come at thy call.'
He biddeth me dream of no rest,
Till I repent that I do best.

[*Lies down and sleeps.*]

Enter WIGGEN, COREBUS, CHURCHWARDEN *and* SEXTON.

Wiggen. You may be ashamed, you whoreson scald Sexton
and Churchwarden (if you had any shame in those   475
shameless faces of yours) to let a poor man lie so long
above ground unburied. A rot on you all, that have no
more compassion of a good fellow when he is gone!
Churchwarden. What, would you have us to bury him, and
to answer it ourselves to the parish?   480

S.D. 468. ERESTUS] *Dyce; Old m.Q.*   471] quotation marks by Bullen.   thy] *Q.;* my *Dyce.*   S.D. 473.1.] *Dyce 1861.*   S.D. 473.2.
COREBUS] (Corobus) *Q.*   S.H. 479. *Churchwarden.*] *Dyce; Simon: Q.*

---

463. *advice*] Q.'s spelling ('advise') gives a guide to pronunciation (to rhyme
with 'wise').

465. *give more than all*] an apparently illogical phrase—though it makes
perfect emotional sense. Greg, in his 'new vampt' version, unnecessarily
'improves' to: 'give part, give all'.

474. *scald*] mean, paltry, contemptible—literally, 'scabby' (one afflicted with
the 'scall'). *O.E.D.* quotes the lines from *OWT* as an illustration.

479. Churchwarden.] Dyce understood Q.'s *Simon* as a mistake for *Steeven*,
the name of the Churchwarden (518). Bullen follows suit, adding, 'Probably the
prefix in the *MS.* was "S".' Hook, p. 349, calls attention to Harold Dowling's
conjecture (*Notes and Queries*, LXIV (1933), p. 184) that 'Simon' may stand for
the name of the actor John Symons, the famous tumbler. See also Chambers,
Eliz. Stage, II, p. 111, for an account of Symons' relation to the Queen's Men.

480. *answer*] to satisfy a pecuniary claim (*O.E.D.*). Hook cites *1H4*,
I.iii.184–5, 'this proud king who studies day and night / To answer all the debt
he owes to you'.

Sexton. Parish me no parishes! Pay me my fees, and let the rest run on in the quarter's accounts, and put it down for one of your good deeds, a God's name; for I am not one that curiously stands upon merits.

Corebus. You whoreson sodden-headed sheep's face! Shall 485 a good fellow do less service and more honesty to the parish, and will you not, when he is dead, let him have Christmas burial?

Wiggen. Peace, Corebus! As sure as Jack was Jack, the frollic'st franion amongst you, and I Wiggen, his 490 sweet sworn brother, Jack shall have his funerals—or some of them shall lie on God's dear earth for it, that's once!

Churchwarden. Wiggen, I hope thou wilt do no more than thou dar'st answer. 495

Wiggen. Sir, sir! dare or dare not! more or less! answer or not answer! do this or have this!

Sexton. Help, help, help! Wiggen sets upon the parish

483. a] *Q.;* o' *Dyce.*   498–9. Wiggen . . . pikestaff] *as Q.; stage direction in Dyce 1861.*

---

482. *the rest run on in*] the remainder (of the cost for burying Jack) be absorbed into.

quarter's accounts] accounts made four times a year.

483. *a God's name*] in God's name.

484. *curiously*] fastidiously.

488. *Christmas*] Corebus' malapropism. He means 'Christian'.

490. *franion*] See 7 n.

491. *sworn brother*] the chivalric custom of two men vowing to share their fate and fortune. See *R2*, V.i.20–1: 'I am sworn brother, sweet, / To grim Necessity'.

491. *funerals*] funeral rites. The use of the plural, in a singular context, derives from Old French *funerailles*.

492–3. *that's once*] that's settled once and for all.

496–7.] Hook compares *Edward I*, 419–21, where action of administering a beating is mirrored in the rhythm of the speech: 'Sir Countriman, kinsman, Englishman, Welshman, you with the Wenche, returne your *Habeas corpus*, heres a *Ciciorari* for your *Precedendo*.'

498–9. *Wiggen . . . pikestaff*] No clarification or improvement seems gained by printing the line as a stage direction. The Sexton is calling out against Wiggen's beating the Churchwarden.

498. *parish*] short for parish official—humorously so, the Sexton regarding

with a pikestaff!

EUMENIDES *awakes and comes to them.*

Eumenides. Hold thy hands, good fellow. 500

Corebus. Can you blame him, sir, if he take Jack's part
against this shake-rotten parish that will not bury
Jack?

Eumenides. Why, what was that Jack?

Corebus. Who, Jack, sir? Who, our Jack, sir? As good a 505
fellow as ever trod upon neat's leather.

Wiggen. Look you, sir; he gave fourscore and nineteen
mourning gowns to the parish when he died, and
because he would not make them up a full hundred,
they would not bury him. Was not this good dealing? 510

Churchwarden. O Lord, sir, how he lies! He was not worth
a halfpenny, and drunk out every penny; and now his
fellows, his drunken companions, would have us to
bury him at the charge of the parish. And we make
many such matches, we may pull down the steeple, 515
sell the bells, and thatch the chancel. He shall lie
above ground till he dance a galliard about the

---

himself as the very symbol of his parish.

502. *shake-rotten*] a phrase not found elsewhere, according to *O.E.D.*, but
obvious in meaning.

506. *trod upon neat's leather*] trod upon = walked about, i.e. he is a good
fellow.

508. *mourning gowns*] No previous editor has annotated the phrase, and I am
indebted to the General Editor for finding this information: 'In 1575 Sir Thomas
Gresham directed in his will that black gowns of cloth at 6s. 8d. the yard were to
be given to a hundred poor men and a hundred poor women to bring him to his
grave; and at Sir Christopher Hatton's funeral in 1592 the bier was preceded by
one hundred poor people whose gowns and caps were given them.' (*Shakespeare's England* (1916), II, p. 149.) In other words, Jack prepared (or Wiggen
invents this) for a funeral befitting an aristocrat; but a tailor had made him, alas,
only ninety-nine, not a hundred gowns for the poor in the parish.

514. *And*] if.

516. *thatch the chancel*] a cheaper replacement for the church's metal or slate
roof, taken down and sold.

517. *galliard*] a quick and lively dance in triple time.

churchyard, for Steven Loach!

Wiggen. Sic argumentaris Domine Loach! 'And we make
many such matches, we may pull down the steeple,   520
sell the bells, and thatch the chancel!' In good time,
sir, and hang yourselves in the bell-ropes when you
have done. *Domine, opponens praepono tibi hanc ques-
tionem*: whether will you have the ground broken, or
your pates broken first? For one of them shall be done   525
presently; and to begin mine, I'll seal it upon your
cockscomb!

Eumenides. Hold thy hands! I pray thee, good fellow, be
not too hasty.

Corebus. [*To* CHURCHWARDEN] You capon's face! We   530
shall have you turned out of the parish one of these
days, with never a tatter to your arse. Then you are in
worse taking than Jack!

Eumenides. Faith, and he is bad enough. This fellow does

---

518. churchyard,] *Dyce subst.;* churchyard *Q.*   519–20. 'And . . . chancel!']
quotation marks by Bullen.   525. broken first? For] *Dyce 1861 subst.;* broken:
first, for *Q.*   528. hands!] *This ed.;* hands, *Q.*   fellow,] *This ed.;* fellow *Q.;*
fellow; *Dyce.*

---

518. *Steven Loach*] the Churchwarden's identification of himself: 'Say I,
Steven Loach.' 'Loach' means simpleton. The expression occurs in *The Merrie
Conceited Jests of George Peele* (1620), p. 26: 'This Loach spares not for any
expence.'

519. Sic . . . Loach] 'Thus you argue, Master Loach': a formula used in
formal disputation.

523–4. Domine . . . questionem] 'Sir, in opposition, I propose to you this
question.'

526. *to begin mine*] Dyce thought that 'some word, or words [may be] wanting
here', but the sense seems clear enough: 'To begin my choice of the "whethers",
I'll vote on the side of a broken pate.'

528–9.] Q.'s comma, after 'hands', indicates that the first clause in the
sentence is separate from the rest and receives an independent emphasis.
Dramatically, the punctuation I suggest seems to have more force than 'Hold
thy hands I pray thee, good fellow! Be not too hasty!' Eumenides interjects with
a sudden, quick exclamation: 'Hold thy hands!'

530. *capon's face*] term of abuse: stupid.

533. *taking*] plight.

but the part of a friend, to seek to bury his friend. 535
How much will bury him?

Wiggen. Faith, about some fifteen or sixteen shillings will
bestow him honestly.

Sexton. Ay, even thereabouts, sir.

Eumenides. Here, hold it, then. [*Aside*] And I have left me 540
but one poor three half-pence. Now do I remember
the words the old man spake at the cross:
'Bestow all thou hast', (and this is all)
'Till dead men's bones comes at thy call.'
Here, hold it. [*Gives money.*] And so, farewell. 545

Wiggen. God, and all good, be with you, sir.

[*Exit* EUMENIDES.]

Nay, you cormorants, I'll bestow one peal of Jack at
mine own proper costs and charges.

Corebus. [*To* CHURCHWARDEN] You may thank God the
long staff and the bilbow blade crossed not your 550
cockscomb.—Well, we'll to the church-stile and have
a pot—and so, trill-lill!

Both. Come, let's go.   *Exeunt.*

---

540. *Aside*] *Dyce 1861.*   543–4.] *as Hook; prose in Q.*   543. 'Bestow . . .
hast,'] *quotation marks by Dyce.*   544.] *quotation marks by Dyce.*   comes]
Q.; come *Dyce.*   S.D. 545. *Gives money*] *Dyce 1861.*   S.D. 546.1. *Exit*
EUMENIDES] *Dyce 1861.*   551. cockscomb] *Q.;* cockscomb *Dyce 1861.*
S.H. 553. *Both.*] *Q.; Church., Sex. Dyce; Wiggen, Corebus conj. Hook.*

---

541. *three half-pence*] a silver coin worth one and a half pennies, issued by
Queen Elizabeth (*O.E.D.*).

547. *cormorants*] traditionally associated with gluttony.

of] on. See *Tw. N.*, III.iv.2: 'How shall I feast him? What bestow of him?'

550. *bilbow blade*] sword made of best Spanish steel.

551. *church-stile*] probably refers to the alehouse adjoining church property.
See Overbury (*Works*, ed. Rimbault (1890), p. 145): 'for at every church stile,
commonly ther's an ale-house'.

552. *trill-lill*] onomatopoeic imitation of the sound of flowing liquid. See
Greene, *James IV* (III.i.17, Revels ed.): 'O sir, the wine runs trillill down his
throat.'

553. Both] Dyce gave the line to the Churchwarden and Sexton, but it seems
more logical to give the line to Corebus and Wiggen, who have just spoken. Of
the four, they leave first.

Fantastic. But, hark you, gammer; methinks this Jack
    bore a great sway in the parish.   555
Madge. O, this Jack was a marvellous fellow. He was but a
    poor man, but very well beloved. You shall see anon
    what this Jack will come to.

Enter the Harvest-men *singing, with women in their hands.*

Frolic. Soft, who have we here? our amorous harvesters.
Fantastic. Ay, ay; let us sit still and let them alone.   560

    Here they begin to sing, the song doubled.

    Lo, here we come a-reaping, a-reaping,
    To reap our harvest fruit;
    And thus we pass the year so long,
    And never be we mute.

                   Exeunt the Harvest-men.

    Enter HUANEBANGO *and* COREBUS *the Clown.*

Frolic. Soft, who have we here?   565
Madge. O, this is a choleric gentleman! All you that love
    your lives, keep out of the smell of his two-hand
    sword. Now goes he to the conjurer.
Fantastic. Methinks the conjurer should put the fool into a
    juggling-box.   570

---

559. harvesters] *Dyce 1861;* harvest starres *Q.;* harvest swains *conj. Blair;*
harvestars *Hook.*   S.D. 564.1. *Exeunt*] *Dyce; Exit Q.*   S.D. 564.2.] *as Q;*
Enter HUANEBANGO *Dyce.*

556–8.] In Greg's 'new vampt' version Jack has been played by Frolic, who at
this point returns to Madge's company. See 351n.
    560.1. doubled] The Harvesters' song and dance take longer than reading the
stage directions indicates. See Intro., pp. 14–15 and 201.1 n.
    564.2.] It is possible, as Dyce and Bullen suggest, to have Corebus enter after
576. Corebus is the 'Booby' of 264–351.
    565. *who have we here?*] On Madge's second introduction of Huanebango, see
Intro., p. 17.
    570. *juggling-box*] meaning uncertain, though the term is associated with
conjuring and legerdemain ('juggling').

Huanebango. Fee, fa, fum,
    Here is the Englishman—
    Conquer him that can—
    Came for his lady bright,
    To prove himself a knight,   575
    And win her love in fight.

Corebus. Who-haw, Master Bango, are you here? Hear
    you, you had best sit down here and beg an alms with
    me.

Huanebango. Hence, base cullion! Here is he that com-   580
    mandeth ingress and egress with his weapon, and will
    enter at his voluntary, whosoever saith no.

    A voice and flame of fire. HUANEBANGO *falleth down.*

Voice. No!

Madge. So with that they kissed and spoiled the edge of as
    good a two-hand sword as ever God put life in. Now   585
    goes Corebus in, spite of the conjurer.

571–2.] *as Dyce; one line in Q.*   573–4.] *as Dyce; one line in Q.*   574. Came]
Q.; Come *Dyce 1861.*   577. Who-haw] *Q. subst.;* Ho, ha! *Dyce 1828.*
S.D. 582.1.] *as Q.; after 583 Dyce 1861.*

571.] traditional war-cry of giants. See Intro., p. 24. Nashe brings in the
refrain in his satire on Gabriel Harvey, but the quotation does not necessarily
prove that Huanebango is meant to be Harvey: 'O, tis a precious apotheg-
maticall Pedant, who will finde matter inough to dilate a whole daye of the first
invention of *Fy, fa, fum*, I smell the bloud of an English-man' (*Works*, III, p.
37). For folk tales in which the cry appears, see 'Jack the Giant-killer' (K.
Briggs, *Dictionary of British Folk Tales*, I, p. 332), 'Jack and the Beanstalk' (p.
318), and 'Childe Rowland' (p. 183). See also *Lr.*, III.iv.179–80: 'Fie, foh, and
fum, / I smell the blood of a British man.'

580. *cullion*] a base, despicable fellow—derived from *coleus* (testicle), as in
Chaucer's *Pardoner's Tale*, 624: 'I wolde I had thy coillons in myn hond.'

580–1. *commandeth ingress and egress*] The gatekeeper with his sword is a
common legendary and mythic figure, from Genesis on: 'So he drove out the
man; and he placed at the east of Eden Cherubims, and a flaming sword which
turned every way, to keep the way of the tree of life' (iii.24). Milton recreates this
ancient image in *Paradise Lost*, XII, 643–4: '[Paradise was] Wav'd over by that
flaming Brand, the Gate / With dreadful Faces throng'd and fierie Armes', and
in *Lycidas*, 130–1: 'that two-handed engine at the door / Stands ready to smite
once, and smite no more'.

582. *at his voluntary*] of his own free will.

Enter [SACRAPANT] *the conjurer* [*and* Two Furies].

Sacrapant. Away with him into the open fields,
     To be a ravening prey to crows and kites.
                    [*Exeunt* Furies *and carry out* HUANEBANGO.]
     And for this villain, let him wander up and down
     In naught but darkness and eternal night.   590

               Strike[s] COREBUS *blind.*

Corebus. Here hast thou slain Huan, a slashing knight,
     And robbèd poor Corebus of his sight.   *Exit.*
Sacrapant. Hence, villain, hence! Now I have unto Delia
     Given a potion of forgetfulness,
     That when she comes she shall not know her
          brothers.   595
     Lo, where they labour like to country slaves,
     With spade and mattock on this enchanted ground.
     Now will I call her by another name,
     For never shall she know herself again,
     Until that Sacrapant hath breathed his last.   600
     See where she comes.

               Enter DELIA.

     Come hither, Delia, take this goad; here hard
     At hand two slaves do work and dig for gold.
     Gore them with this, and thou shalt have enough.

               He gives her a goad.

Delia. Good sir, I know not what you mean.   605

S.D. 586.1. *and* Two Furies] *Dyce 1861.*   S.D. 588.1.] *as Hook;* HUAN *is
carried out by the* Two Furies *Dyce 1861.*   S.D. 590.1.] *as Dyce 1861; after
586.1. in Q.   Strikes*] *Dyce; strike Q.   592. Exit*] *as Q.; after* hence! 593
Dyce 1861.   593–4.] *as Dyce;* Hence . . . hence. / Now . . . forgetfulness *Q.
602–3.] as Dyce;* Come . . . gode, / Here . . . gold *Q.*

     586.1. and *Two Furies*] It is obvious that Sacrapant is addressing attendant
spirits here, and needs their help to carry out Huanebango.
     596. *labour*] The enforced labour motif has been common since the story of
the labours of Herakles. See, for instance, 'The Swan Maiden' (Pyle, *The
Wonder Clock*, pp. 234–38). Shakespeare uses the motif in *Tp.*, III.i.

Sacrapant. [*Aside*] She hath forgotten to be Delia,

But not forgot the same she should forget.

But I will change her name.—

Fair Berecynthia (so this country calls you)

Go ply these strangers, wench; they dig for gold.   610

Exit SACRAPANT.

Delia. O heavens! how am I beholding to this fair young
man.

But I must ply these strangers to their work.

See where they come.

Enter the Two Brothers *in their shirts, with spades, digging.*

First Brother. O brother, see where Delia is!

Second Brother. O Delia, happy are we to see thee here!   615

Delia. What tell you me of Delia, prating swains?

I know no Delia, nor know I what you mean.

Ply you your work or else you are like to smart.

First Brother. Why, Delia, knowst thou not thy brothers
here?

We come from Thessaly to seek thee forth;   620

And thou deceiv'st thyself, for thou art Delia.

Delia. Yet more of Delia? Then take this and smart!

S.D. 606. *Aside*] *Dyce 1861*.   607. same] *Q.;* name *Hook*.   611.] *as Q.;* O
. . . to / This . . . man *Dyce 1828;* O . . . how / Am . . . man *Dyce 1861*.
615.] *as Q.;* O Delia / Happy . . . here *Dyce 1861*.   618. you are] *Q.;* you're
Dyce 1861.

607.] I fail to see why this line gives difficulty or why emendation has been
thought necessary. A loose paraphrase of Sacrapant's speech (606–8) is: 'My
charms have worked so far in that Delia has forgotten her identity as Delia, but
not to the extent that she has forgotten what she should forget—i.e. her loyalty
to her brothers and her aversion to me. By giving her another name (Berecynthia) I hope I can completely change her sense of identity.'

Gummere reads 607 similarly: 'Sacrapant says [Delia] has forgotten her name,
but has not forgotten as much as she ought to forget.' Hook emends to 'name'
and paraphrases thus: 'Delia, while still responding to the name, has forgotten
everything else about herself.'

609. *Berecynthia*] one of the names for Cybele, the goddess of the earth, as in
Aeneid, VI, 785: '*Berecynthia mater*'.

611. *beholding*] beholden, as in *Mer. V.*, I.iii.100: 'Well, Shylock, shall we be
beholding to you?'

[Pricks them with the goad.]

What feign you shifts for to defer your labour?
Work, villains, work; it is for gold you dig!

Second Brother. Peace, brother, peace; this vild enchanter   625
Hath ravished Delia of her senses clean,
And she forgets that she is Delia.

First Brother. Leave, cruel thou, to hurt the miserable.
Dig, brother, dig; for she is hard as steel.

Here they dig and descry the light under a little hill.

Second Brother. Stay, brother! What hast thou descried?   630
Delia. Away, and touch it not! It is something that
My lord hath hidden there.

She covers it again.

Enter SACRAPANT.

Sacrapant. Well said! Thou plyest these pioneers well.
Go get you in, you labouring slaves!

[Exeunt the Two Brothers.]

Come, Berecynthia, let us in likewise,   635
And hear the nightingale record her notes.   *Exeunt.*

Enter ZANTIPPA, *the Curst Daughter, to the well, with a pot in her
hand.*

S.D. 622.1.]*Dyce 1861.*   625. vild]*Q.;* vile*Dyce 1861.*   631–2. that / My]
Dyce 1861; prose in Q.; some thing, / That *Hook.*   631. It is] *Q. subst.;* 'tis
Dyce 1861.   633–4. well. / Go]*Dyce 1861 subst.; prose in Q.*   S.D. 634.1.]
Dyce 1861.   S.D. 636. Exeunt] *Dyce 1861; Exeunt omnes Q.*

---

625. *vild*] early form of 'vile'. (In *Ant.*, V. ii.312, Folio's 'this wilde world' is
probably a misprint for 'vilde'. See *Lr.*, III.vii.82: 'Out, vilde gelly'.)

629.1. descry] See Intro., p. 11 and n. 33.

633. *Well said*] possibly equivalent to 'Well done', as in Dekker, *Westward
Ho*, II.ii.67; but the words may also be taken literally, i.e. Sacrapant praises
Delia for her harsh words to her brothers.

636.1. well] See R. C. Hope's *Holy Wells: their Legends and Traditions* (London, 1893), pp. 187–93, for an example of a maiden seeking out the well for a
solution to 'matters of love'.

Zantippa. Now for a husband, house and home! God send
a good one or none, I pray God! My father hath sent
me to the well for the water of life, and tells me if I
give fair words I shall have a husband.   640

> *Enter* [CELANTA] *the Foul Wench, to the well for water,*
> *with a pot in her hand.*

But here comes Celanta, my sweet sister. I'll stand by
and hear what she says.   [*Withdraws.*]
Celanta. My father hath sent me to the well for water; and
he tells me if I speak fair, I shall have a husband, and
none of the worst. Well, though I am black, I am sure 645
all the world will not forsake me; and, as the old
proverb is: Though I am black I am not the devil.
Zantippa. [*Approaching.*] Marry-gup with a murrain! I
know wherefore thou speakest that; but go thy ways
home as wise as thou cam'st, or I'll set thee home with 650
a wanion!

> *Here she strikes her pitcher against her sister's, and breaks them both*
> *and goes her way.*

Celanta. I think this be the curstest quean in the world.
You see what she is—a little fair, but as proud as the

S.D. 640.1–2.] *as Q.; after 642, Dyce 1861.*   S.D. 642. *Withdraws*] *This ed.;*
Retires Dyce 1861.   S.D. 648. *Approaching*] *This ed.; coming forward Dyce*
1861.   murrain] (murren) *Q.*   S.H. 652. *Celanta.*] (*Clant.*) *Q.*

---

645. *black*] dark-complexioned—hence, by implication, ugly—as beautiful
ladies were traditionally fair and blond.

647. *proverb*] Tilley, D297, quotes Greene's *Quip for an Upstart Courtier*, ed.
Grosart, XI, p. 259: 'Marry quoth hee, that lookte like Lucifer, though I am
blacke I am not the Divell, but indeed a Colier of Croiden.'

648. *Marry-gup*] exclamatory phrase, often of derision (*O.E.D.*).

murrain] plague. Zantippa's imprecation means 'Plague take you!'

650–1. *with a wanion*] with a plague, with a vengeance. a variant of 'waniad',
the time of the waning of the moon, an unlucky hour. In Dekker's *Shoemaker's*
Holiday the phrase is combined with 'marry-gup': 'Mary gup thought I with a
wanion' (I.ii.31).

652. *quean*] hussy.

devil, and the veriest vixen that lives upon God's
earth. Well, I'll let her alone, and go home and get　655
another pitcher, and, for all this, get me to the well
for water.　　　　　　　　　　　　　　　　　*Exit.*

Enter Two Furies *out of the conjurer's cell, and lays*
　　　　HUANEBANGO *by the well of life.*
　　　Enter ZANTIPPA *with a pitcher to the well.*

Zantippa. Once again for a husband! and, in faith,
Celanta, I have got the start of you! Belike husbands
grow by the well-side. Now my father says I must rule　660
my tongue. Why, alas, what am I then? A woman
without a tongue is as a soldier without his weapon.
But I'll have my water and be gone.

Here she offers to dip her pitcher in, and a Head *speaks in the well.*

Head. Gently dip, but not too deep,
　　For fear you make the golden bird to weep.　　　　665

S.D. 657.1. *lays*] Q. *subst.; lay Dyce.*　　　S.D. 663.1. *speaks*] Q.; *rises Dyce*
1861.　　665. *bird*] *Q.; beard Dyce.*

663.1. *speaks*] I retain Q., though it is obvious that the Head 'rises' at this
point. For an account of the tradition behind the action, see Ann Ross, 'Severed
Heads in Wells: an Aspect of the Well Cult', *Scottish Studies,* VI, 1962, pp.
31–48. (See also Intro., pp. 21–2.)

665. *bird*] Dyce, and all editors since, emend to *beard*, and similarly follow the
corrected quarto readings at 813 and 818. One may suppose that for the two later
passages, both on sig. E4 in quarto, the proof-reader decided, as have modern
editors, that *bird* did not make sense and that *beard* fitted the context more
logically. The Head at 816.1 is combed for gold: golden hair, golden beard.
Also, as Hook points out (813 n.), *beard* can be understood as metonymy for the
Head itself. The Head rising from the well, especially in the later episode (817
ff.), when golden riches are poured into Celanta's lap, is symbolic of harvest and
fertility. The 'beard' is part of the sheaf of wheat (821–2).

Hook suggests that one would 'not expect the correction to *beard* (at 813 and
818) without recourse to manuscript' (p. 379). But it is difficult to see how *beard*
in the manuscript copy could have been misread as *bird* three times, and
moreover by two different compositors (see Intro., pp. 8 and 10). The proof-
reader's reasons, therefore, were probably different, and without authority.

I follow the quarto reading (and uncorrected quarto at 813 and 818) because it
makes as good sense as the emendation. The reference, then, is to an unspecified
'golden bird' (the phoenix?) of magical powers. The lines chanted by the Head

Fair maiden, white and red,
Stroke me smooth, and comb my head,
And thou shalt have some cockell-bread.
Zantippa. What is this?
   'Fair maiden, white and red,   670
   Comb me smooth, and stroke my head,
   And thou shalt have some cockell-bread.'
   'Cockell' callest thou it, boy? Faith, I'll give you
cockell-bread!

She breaks her pitcher upon his head; then it thunders and

669–70.] *as Dyce; one line in Q.*   670–2.] *quotation marks by Dyce 1861.*
673. 'Cockell'] *quotation marks by Dyce 1861.*   S.D. 674.1. *his head*] *Q.; the*
Head *Dyce 1861.*

---

are in the nature of a 'charm', and it is not necessary that *bird* be logical, the 'primary associations of charm [being] with music, sound and rhythm' rather than with sense and reason (see Northrop Frye, 'Charms and Riddles', *Spiritus Mundi*, 1976, pp. 123–47). Peele's intention was to convey poetic sound and a sense of mystery.

  No decision, however, can be arrived at with any certainty. The reader should decide on his own preference for either *bird* or *beard*.

  668. *cockell-bread*] John Aubrey's manuscript for *Remaines of Gentilisme and Judaisme* (Lansdowne MSS 231) gives a clear and frank account of the rustic 'wanton sport' of 'moulding cockle-bread', which leaves no doubt as to what the Head is saying to Zantippa, or to why she should give the Head a clout for his bawdy teasing: 'Young wenches have a wanton sport, which they call moulding of Cocklebread; viz. they gett upon a Table-board, and then gather-up their knees & their coates with their hands as high as they can, and then they wabble to and fro with the Buttocks as if the[y] were kneading of Dowgh with their A——, and say these words, viz:
            My Dame is sick & gonne to bed,
            And I'le go mowld my cockle-bread'
                    (ed. Britten, for the Folk Lore Society, p. 43).
Dyce, and others who base their editions on his work, refer to Aubrey, but still profess themselves puzzled by what the term means. By delicately editing out certain of Aubrey's earthy phrases, and by missing the basic *double entendre* in the name of the 'sport' itself, the closest they get to a definition is that the phrase is used as 'a love charm'.

> *lightens, and* HUANEBANGO *rises up.* HUANEBANGO *is*
> *deaf and cannot hear.*

Huanebango. Philida phileridos, pamphilida florida 675
    flortos,

Dub dub-a-dub, bounce, quoth the guns, with a
    sulphurous huff-snuff!

Waked with a wench, pretty peat, pretty love, and
    my sweet pretty pigsnie.

Just by thy side shall sit surnamèd great Huane-
    bango;

Safe in my arms will I keep thee, threat Mars or
    thunder Olympus!

Zantippa. Foh! what greasy groom have we here? He looks 680
    as though he crept out of the backside of the well, and

674.2. HUANEBANGO rises up] The hilarious episode of Huanebango's 'resurrection' is seldom considered for its comic merits, but is looked at from the point
of view that Huanebango exists to parody Gabriel Harvey. The attempts to find
links between Harvey and Huanebango in this episode begin with the stage
direction at 674.3: HUANEBANGO *is deaf* ('Harvey had an indifferent ear for verse,
and here, perhaps—since the hexameters [parodying Harvey] follow so hard
upon—is a neat way of stating the fact' (Gummere)). Huanebango's exit line
(716–17) has also been interpreted as mocking Harvey, who was supposedly
always trying to overcompensate for his humble birth. But to see Huanebango
only as a parody of Harvey is to limit the richness of the character.

675.] Spanish-sounding nonsense.

676.] a parody of Richard Stanyhurst's 'hexameter furie' (Nashe, III, p. 319)
in his translation of *Aeneid*:

Lowd dub a dub tabering with frapping rip rap of Aetna.
Theare stroakes stronglye threshing, yawl furth groans, stamped on anvyl.

                    (E. Arber, ed., *English Scholar's Library*, (1895), X, p. 137)

huff-snuff] See Stanyhurst's 'Of a Craking Cutter': 'Linckt was in wedlock a
loftye Thrasonical huf snuffe' (Arber, *op. cit.*, p. 143). Gabriel Harvey used the
expression in *Greenes Memorial* (Sonnet VI): 'I wott not what these cutting
Huffe-snuffes meane' (*Works*, ed. Grosart, 1884, vol. I, p. 241); and Nashe
threw the phrase back at Harvey in his lampoon of him in *Foure Letters Confuted*
(I, p. 300): 'But ah what newes doe you heare of that good Gabriel huffe snuffe, /
Knowne to the world for a foole, and clapt in the Fleet for a Rimer?' Peele is
probably parodying both Stanyhurst and Harvey, joining with Nashe in mocking Harvey in retaliation for his words against Greene.

677. *peat*] term of endearment; pet of a woman.

pigsnie] one specially cherished; a darling, pet.

speaks like a drum perished at the west end.

Huanebango. O that I might, but I may not; woe to my
destiny therefore.

Kiss that I clasp, but I cannot; tell me, my destiny,
wherefore?

Zantippa. [*Aside*] Whoop! Now I have my dream! Did you   685
never hear so great a wonder as this? Three blue
beans in a blue bladder—rattle, bladder, rattle!

Huanebango. I'll now set my countenance, and to her in
prose. It may be this rim ram ruff is too rude an
encounter.—Let me, fair lady (if you be at leisure)   690

S.D. 685. *Aside*] *Dyce 1861.*   689. rim] *QB, QH;* rude *QD, QP.*   690. Let]
indented two spaces in Q.

---

682. *perished at the west end*] i.e. broken. But I have been unable to discover
the precise meaning of the phrase.

683.] As Dyce noted, the line is a quotation from Harvey's '*Ecomium Lauri*'
(1580):
> Faine wod I crave, might I so presume, some farther aquaintaunce,
> O that I might? but I may not: woe to my destinie therefore.
>
> (*Works, ed. cit.,* I, p. 82)

686–7. *Three blue beans . . . rattle*] proverbial. See Dekker, *Old Fortunatus,*
I.ii.165, and Jonson's *Bartholomew Fair,* I.iv.76. The phrase occurs in Alleyn's
part in *Orlando Furioso,* which may be further evidence of connection between
Greene's play and *OWT.* See Intro., p. 5, and 890–3 n.

> . . . lett him put his arme into
> my bagg [t]hus deep, yf he will eate g[old]
> he shall have it. thre blew bean[s]
> a blewe bladder, rattle, bladder rattle

(lines 134–7 of Alleyn MS, in W. G. Greg, *Dramatic Documents,* 1931, vol. II)

689. *rim ram ruff*] '*Rude* ram ruffe' in the uncorrected copies QD and QP is
likely the compositor's anticipation of 'too *rude* an encounter'. The phrase
originates with Chaucer, *Parson's Prologue,* 43: 'I am a Southren man, / I can nat
geste—rum, ram, ruf—by lettre.' The Parson means that he is not skilled in
fancy, alliterative language. (Alliterative poems were usually in the Northern, or
West Midland, dialect (Skeat, *Works of Chaucer,* V, p. 445).) Peele is again
satirising Stanyhurst's alliterative hexameters:
> Now doe they rayse gastly lyghtnings, now grislye reboundings
> Or ruffe raffe roaring, mens herts with terror agrysing.
>
> (Arber, *op. cit.,* p. 138)

Nashe and Barnaby Rich likewise used variations of the phrase in parodying
Stanyhurst:
> Then did he make heavens vault to rebound, with rounce robble hobble
> Of ruffe raffe roaring, with thwicke thwacke thurlerie bouncing
>
> (Nashe, III, p. 320)

revel with your sweetness, and rail upon that
cowardly conjurer that hath cast me (or congealed
me, rather) into an unkind sleep and polluted my
carcass.

Zantippa. Laugh, laugh, Zantippa! Thou hast thy for-   695
tune—a fool and a husband under one.

Huanebango. Truly, sweetheart, as I seem—about some
twenty years, the very April of mine age.

Zantippa. [*Aside*] Why, what a prating ass is this!

Huanebango. Her coral lips, her crimson chin,   700
Her silver teeth so white within,
Her golden locks, her rolling eye,
Her pretty parts—let them go by—
Heigh-ho, hath wounded me,
That I must die this day to see.   705

Zantippa. By gog's bones, thou art a flouting knave! 'Her
coral lips, her crimson chin!' Ka, wilshaw!

Huanebango. True, my own, and my own because mine,
and mine because mine—ha, ha! Above a thousand
pounds in possibility and things fitting thy desire in   710
possession.

S.D. 699. *Aside*] *Dyce 1861*.   704. hath *Q.*, have *Dyce*.   706–7. 'Her . . .
chin!'] *quotation marks by Dyce 1861*.

'. . . he tooke upon him to translate *Virgill*, and stript him out of a Velvet gowne,
into a Fooles coat, out of a Latin Heroicall verse, into an English riffe raffe'
(Rich, quoted in Arber, *op. cit.*, p. viii).

690–1. *Let . . . revel*] The line is indented in Q., making two paragraphs of
Huanebango's speech. Hook suggests, 'This may be a way of indicating that the
preceding sentence is an aside.'

700–5.] In *MND*, V.i.321–3, courtly feature-by-feature praise of a fair lady is
similarly ridiculed by being put in the mouth of a clown:

These lily lips,
This cherry nose,
These yellow cowslip cheeks.

706. *gog's*] a corrupt form of 'God's' employed in oaths.
flouting] mocking, jeering.
707. *Ka, wilshaw*] meaning unknown. 'Ka' (*O.E.D.* and Skeat and Mayhew,
Glossary of Tudor and Stuart Words) is a form of 'quoth, quotha (i.e. quoth he)'.
Gummere suggests 'Will ich ha[v]e' for 'wilshaw'.

Zantippa. [*Aside*] The sot thinks I ask of his lands. Lob be
    your comfort, and cuckold be your destiny!—Hear
    you, sir: and if you will have us you had best say so
    betime.   715
Huanebango. True, sweetheart, and will royalize thy
    progeny with my pedigree!   *Exeunt omnes.*

     Enter EUMENIDES *the Wandering Knight.*

Eumenides. Wretched Eumenides, still unfortunate,
    Envied by Fortune, and forlorn by Fate;
    Here pine and die, wretched Eumenides.   720
    Die in the spring, the April of my age?
    Here sit thee down, repent what thou hast done.
    I would to God that it were ne'er begun.

           Enter JACK.

Jack. You are well overtaken, sir.
Eumenides. Who's that?   725
Jack. You are heartily well met, sir.

S.D. 712. *Aside*] *Dyce 1861.*   717. pedigree] (petigree) *Q.*   721. my age?]
Q.; thy age! *Dyce;* my age! *Neilson.*   S.D. 723.1. JACK] (Iacke) *Q.; the Ghost
of* JACK *Dyce 1861.*   S.H. 724. *Jack.*] (*Iacke:*) *Q.; G. of Jack, passim, Dyce
1861.*   725. Who's] *QB, QH;* Whose *QD, QP.*

712. *Lob*] clown, lout. Hook paraphrases: 'Zantippa's kindly wish for
Huanebango is . . . that his destiny as a cuckold may be somewhat mitigated by
his being too much a simpleton to recognize the horror of his fate.'
   714. *us*] Zantippa uses the royal plural. She is a proud and self-centred as
Huanebango. A perfect match.
   721.] It is not necessary to emend. If the line is read as a question, one sees
Eumenides suddenly stopping in his ritual lament, with a personal recognition
of his situation. The 'April of my age' phrase, made ridiculous by Huanebango
(698), is serious now, as it was when spoken by Erestus (201).
   723.1.] The *peripeteia* caused by Jack's appearance resembles the plot structure of fairy tales—at those moments in which the miraculous appearance of
what will bring the solution occurs just at the hero's lowest point. The stylized,
'contrived' effect is intentional. (To insert *The Ghost of* before JACK is needlessly
pedantic and destroys the suspense as to the true nature of Jack.)
   724–9.] Jack is 'invisible' here. His pinching is a common trick of unseen
spirits. He materialises after 729.

Eumenides. Forbear, I say! Who is that which pincheth me?

Jack. Trusting in God, good Master Eumenides, that you are in so good health as all your friends were at the   730
making hereof. God give you God-morrow, sir. Lack you not a neat, handsome, and cleanly young lad, about the age of fifteen or sixteen years, that can run by your horse, and, for a need, make your master-ship's shoes as black as ink? How say you, sir?   735

Eumenides. Alas, pretty lad, I know not how to keep myself—and much less a servant, my pretty boy, my state is so bad.

Jack. Content yourself, you shall not be so ill a master but I'll be as bad a servant. Tut, sir, I know you, though   740
you know not me. Are you not the man, sir (deny it if you can, sir) that came from a strange place in the land of Catita, where Jackanapes flies with his tail in his mouth, to seek out a lady as white as snow and as red as blood? Ha, ha! have I touched you now?   745

731. God-morrow] *Q. subst.;* good morrow *Dyce.*

---

731. *making*] Hook glosses 'at the conception of Eumenides' and quotes *2H4*, III.ii.312–13: Justice Shallow is 'like a man made after supper of a cheese paring'. But the meaning is surely 'Trusting . . . that you are in as good health as that "made" for you when your friends drank your health.'

733–4. *run by your horse*] i.e. as a foot page.

734. *for a need*] when you need.

741–2. *man, sir . . . can, sir*] Gummere notes that the 'rhyming scraps' are akin to 'formula jingles in popular tales'. See 146 n.

743. *Catita*] i.e. some fabulous land. No source for the name has been discovered, and Peele may have invented it. Marston also couples 'land of Catito' and 'Jackanapes' in *The Malcontent*, I.iii.55–9 (Revels edn.): 'dreams, dreams, visions, fantasies, chimeras, imaginations, tricks, conceits! . . . Sir Tristram Trimtram, come aloft Jack-an-apes with a whim-wham: here's a Knight of the land of Catito shall play at trap with any page of Europe.' G. K. Hunter in his note there gives *O.W.T.* as Marston's source and cites Kittredge's suggestion that *Catito* comes from *cat*, a card game, like *trap*. This interpretation fits *The Malcontent* better than *O.W.T.*

Jackanapes] Though the precise origin of the word is uncertain (it perhaps began as 'an approbrious nickname of William de la Pole' (1450), whose badge displayed an ape (*O.E.D.*)), it was used in Elizabethan times to describe a man whose airs made him ridiculous, like a monkey—or, 'playfully, a pert, forward child, a "monkey"' (*O.E.D.*). This sounds somewhat like Jack himself.

Eumenides. [*Aside*] I think this boy be a spirit.—How
    knowst thou all this?

Jack. Tut, are you not the man, sir (deny it if you can, sir)
    that gave all the money you had to the burying of a
    poor man, and but one three half-pence left in your   750
    purse? Content you, sir, I'll serve you, that is flat.

Eumenides. Well, my lad, since thou art so importunate, I
    am content to entertain thee—not as a servant, but a
    copartner in my journey. But whither shall we go? for
    I have not any money more than one bare three   755
    half-pence.

Jack. Well, master, content yourself; for if my divination
    be not out, that shall be spent at the next inn or
    alehouse we come to. For, master, I know you are
    passing hungry. Therefore I'll go before and provide   760
    dinner until that you come. No doubt but you'll come
    fair and softly after.

Eumenides. Ay, go before; I'll follow thee.

Jack. But do you hear, master? Do you know my name?

Eumenides. No, I promise thee, not yet.   765

Jack. Why, I am Jack.   *Exit* JACK.

Eumenides. Jack. Why, be it so, then.

> *Enter the* HOSTESS *and* JACK, *setting meat on the table,*
> *and Fiddlers come to play.* EUMENIDES *walketh up and*
> *down, and will eat no meat.*

Host. How say you, sir? Do you please to sit down?

Eumenides. Hostess, I thank you; I have no great stomach.

Host. [*To* JACK] Pray, sir, what is the reason your master is   770
    so strange? Doth not this meat please him?

Jack. Yes, hostess, but it is my master's fashion to pay
    before he eats. Therefore, a reckoning, good hostess.

S.D. 746. *Aside*] *Dyce 1861*.   746–7.] *as Dyce;* I . . . spirit,] How . . . this? *Q*.
752. importunate] *Dyce*; impornate *Q*.   766. *Exit*] *Dyce; Exeunt Q*.   S.D.
767.2. *come*] *Dyce*; came *Q*.

    769. *stomach*] appetite.

Host. Marry shall you, sir, presently.   *Exit.*

Eumenides. Why, Jack, what dost thou mean? Thou   775
    knowest I have not any money. Therefore, sweet
    Jack, tell me what shall I do?

Jack. Well, master, look in your purse.

Eumenides. Why, faith, it is a folly, for I have no money.

Jack. Why, look you, master; do so much for me.   780

Eumenides. Alas, Jack, my purse is full of money.

Jack. 'Alas!' Master, does that word belong to this acci-
    dent? Why, methinks I should have seen you cast
    away your cloak, and in a bravado danced a galliard
    round about the chamber. Why, master, your man   785
    can teach you more wit than this. Come, hostess;
    cheer up my master!

[*Enter* HOSTESS.]

Hostess. You are heartily welcome. And if it please you to
    eat of a fat capon, a fairer bird, a finer bird, a sweeter
    bird, a crisper bird, a neater bird, your worship never   790
    eat of.

Eumenides. Thanks, my fine, eloquent hostess.

Jack. But hear you, master, one word by the way. Are you

782. 'Alas!'] *quotation marks by Dyce 1861.*   784. danced] (daunced) *Q.;*
dance *Dyce.*   S.D. 787.1.] *Dyce subst.*   791. of] *Dyce;* off *Q.*

---

774. *shall you, sir, presently*] You shall have it at once, sir.

781. *Alas . . . money*] Not an exclamation. The bewildered and tired
Eumenides speaks in a flat tone of voice.

784. *bravado*] with a flourish, in a brave style, splendidly.

789–90. *fairer bird . . . neater bird*] Hook compares the lines of Dandaline the
Hostess in *Liberality and Prodigality*, 1602:
        A better bird, a fairer bird, a finer bird,
        A sweeter bird, a yonger bird, a tenderer bird,
        A daintier bird, a crisper bird, a more delicate bird,
        Was there never set upon any Gentlemans board.
                         (*Malone Society Reprints*, 519–22)
But as *Liberality and Prodigality* may be an early Elizabethan play revived before
the Queen in 1601, one cannot be sure of the indebtedness of the passage to
Peele.

791. *eat*] past tense; pronounced 'et'. See *O.E.D.*

content I shall be halves in all you get in your jour-
ney? 795
Eumenides. I am, Jack; here is my hand.
Jack. Enough, master; I ask no more.
Eumenides. Come, hostess, receive your money; and I
thank you for my good entertainment.
Hostess. You are heartily welcome, sir. 800
Eumenides. Come, Jack, whither go we now?
Jack. Marry, master, to the conjurer's presently.
Eumenides. Content, Jack. Hostess, farewell.

Exe[*unt*] *om*[*nes*].

Enter COREBUS [*blind*] *and* CELANTA *the Foul Wench*
to the well for water.

Corebus. Come, my duck, come. I have now got a wife.
Thou art fair, art thou not? 805
Celanta. My Corebus, the fairest alive; make no doubt of
that.
Corebus. Come, wench, are we almost at the well?
Celanta. Ay, Corebus, we are almost at the well now. I'll
go fetch some water. Sit down while I dip my pitcher 810
in.
Voice. Gently dip, but not too deep,
For fear you make the golden bird to weep.

A Head *comes up with ears of corn, and she combs them in her lap.*

Fair maiden, white and red,
Comb me smooth, and stroke my head, 815

S.D. 803.2. *blind*] *Neilson.* CELANTA] *Dyce;* Zelanto *Q.*   S.H. 806. *Celanta.*]
Dyce; Zelan: *Q., passim to* 828 (Zela: *at* 809).   S.H. 812. *Voice*] *Q.;* Head
Dyce 1861.   813. bird] *QD, QP;* beard *QB, QH.*   S.D. 813.1.] *as Q.;*
after 811, *Dyce 1861.*

803.1. CELANTA] One can only guess why in Q. Celanta's name in this episode
(to 830) is changed to Zelanto: by Peele inadvertently? By a scribe? Hook (p.
349) mentions the further possibility of the compositor misreading MS, but *C*
can hardly be misread as *Z.*
   813, 818. bird] See 665 n.
   813.1.] Dyce (1861) wrongly places the S.D. after 811. The mysterious voice
from the well is heard before the Head appears. See S.D. 663.1.

And thou shalt have some cockell-bread. [*Descends.*]

A Head *comes up full of gold; she combs it into her lap.*

Gently dip, but not too deep,
For fear thou make the golden bird to weep.
Fair maiden, white and red,
Comb me smooth, and stroke my head;   820
And every hair a sheaf shall be,
And every sheaf a golden tree.   [*Descends.*]

Celanta. O see, Corebus! I have combed a great deal of
    gold into my lap, and a great deal of corn.
Corebus. Well said, wench! Now we shall have tost 825
    enough. God send us coiners to coin our gold. But
    come, shall we go home, sweetheart?
Celanta. Nay, come, Corebus; I will lead you.
Corebus. So, Corebus, things have well hit;
    Thou hast gotten wealth to mend thy wit.   *Exeunt.* 830

Enter JACK *and* [EUMENIDES] *the Wandering Knight.*

S.D. 816.1.]*as Dyce 1861; after* 822,*Q.; after* 818, *Hook.*   S.D. 816.1. Head]
Q.; Second Head Dyce.   818. bird] *QD, QP;* beard *QB, QH.*   819.
maiden] *Hook;* maide *Q.*   821, 822. sheaf] *Dyce;* sheave *Q.*   825. tost]
QD, QP; iust *QB, QH;* grist *conj. Bullen;* toast *conj. Daniel.*   826. coiners]
QB, QH; quoiners *QD, QP.*   coin] *QB, QH* (coine)*; quine QD,
QP.*   S.D. 830. *Exeunt*] *Dyce; Exit Q.*

___

818. *thou*] Peele may not have intended the change in form of address to
Celanta (from 'you' in 813) to have great significance, but the effect of the change
is to point up the Head's grateful, friendly and benevolent attitude toward
kindly Celanta.

825. *tost*] tossed? toast? See Intro., p. 9. If 'tost' is wrong, no satisfactory
alternative has been suggested by editors, and by not following other editors in
printing 'just', at least one stage in the corrupted reading is eliminated. Daniel
(in Bullen edn., I, p. 340) may be right that Corebus refers to toast (spelled 'tost'
in Q. at line 964) or he may refer to Celanta having tossed corn and gold into her
lap. But the reading remains suspect.

826. *coiners . . . coin*] Hook takes this to be the printer's modernisation: 'One
must assume that the copy preserved the archaic form ['quoiners . . . quine']; it
is unlikely that the printer, whose general tendency is toward modernising,
would have set an archaic form if his copy had the modern form.' See also Intro.,
pp. 9–10, for a possible pun on quoiner = corner-stone maker.

Jack. Come away, master, come.

Eumenides. Go along, Jack; I'll follow thee. Jack, they say
    it is good to go cross-legged and say his prayers
    backward. How sayest thou?

Jack. Tut, never fear, master; let me alone. Here sit you   835
    still; speak not a word. And because you shall not be
    enticed with his enchanting speeches, with this same
    wool I'll stop your ears. [*Puts wool into* EUMENIDES'
    ears.] And so, master, sit still; for I must to the
    conjurer.   *Exit* JACK.   840

    Enter [SACRAPANT] *the Conjurer to* [EUMENIDES] *the
                Wandering Knight.*

Sacrapant. How now! What man art thou that sits so sad?
    Why dost thou gaze upon these stately trees
    Without the leave and will of Sacrapant?

---

833. his prayers] *Q.;* prayers *Dyce.*   S.D. 838–9. *Puts . . . ears*] *Dyce subst.*

833–4. *go cross legged . . . say his prayers backward*] These ritual motions often
associated with bad luck and the summoning of evil forces can bring favourable
fortune as well. Although 'Juno sitting cross-legged prevents Alcmena's deliv-
ery [in childbirth] ' (Lean, *Collectanea*, 1904, II, p. 111), conversely:

    Run to Love's Lottery, run maids and rejoice—
    Whilst seeking your chance, you meet your choice,—
    And boast that your luck you help with design,
    By praying cross-legged to Saint Valentine.

                                         (Lean, II, p. 404)

Saying prayers backward conjures up the devil (Lean, II, p. 430), but on the
other hand can undo evil spells. Gummere cites *Comus*:

    What, have you let the false enchanter scape?
    O ye mistook; ye should have snatcht his wand
    And bound him fast; without his rod revers't,
    And backward mutters of dissevering power,
    We cannot free the Lady . . .

                                         (813–17)

833. *his*] one's.

836. *because you*] in order that you.

838. *stop your ears*] The motif is as ancient as the *Odyssey* (XII, 177), where
Odyssus stops his companions' ears against the Sirens' enchanting songs.

What! not a word but mum?
Then, Sacrapant, thou art betrayed.   845

Enter JACK, *invisible, and taketh off* SACRAPANT'S
wreath from his head, and his sword out of his hand.

What hand invades the head of Sacrapant?
What hateful Fury doth envy my happy state?
Then, Sacrapant, these are thy latest days.
Alas, my veins are numbed, my sinews shrink,
My blood is pierced, my breath fleeting away;   850
And now my timeless date is come to end.
He in whose life his actions hath been so foul,
Now in his death to hell descends his soul.

He dieth [*and his body is removed*].

844–5. mum?/Then] *Q. subst.;* mum? Then, Sacrapant, / Thou *Dyce 1861.*
847. What hateful Fury] *Q. subst.;* What Fury *conj. Dyce.*   850. pierced]
(pearst) *Q.;* iced *conj. Daniel.*   852. life his] *Q.;* life's *conj. Neilson.*   actions hath] *Q.;* actions have *Dyce 1828;* acts have *Dyce 1861;* acts hath
Bullen.

---

844. *not a word but mum*] proverbial. See Tilley, W767. Logic does not strictly
apply here, for (as far as the audience knows) Sacrapant has not been told to fear
a silent man. But, in the level of mythic realism, the audience accepts this new
revelation of Sacrapant's vulnerability. Eumenides' 'dangerous silence' has been
part of tradition from the Sphinx to the Tar Baby.

845.1. Enter JACK] From Jack's sudden entrance here, until the very end of
the play, the action is as swift, jumbled, and full of quick reversals, as when
Madge first began her tale—even though the characters seemed at first to be
organising things a bit better when they stepped in to tell Madge's tale for her.
The natural, jubilant spirit of folk tale governs the final movement of the play.
Rational order is not expected.

847.] Bullen suggests that 'as the metre of this play is regular, either "hateful"
or "happy" should be expunged'. But the metre is not always regular, and in this
case, as Hook comments, 'the alliteration and the contrasting adjectives suggest
that rhetoric prevailed over metre'. 'Envy' is accented on the second syllable
(rhymes with 'imply').

850. *blood*] If 'blood' is understood to mean 'life' (*O.E.D.*, II, 4) one need not
query 'pierced'.

851. *timeless date*] everlasting life. See *Per.*, III.iv.14: 'Where you may abide
till your date expire.' 'Timeless . . . come to end' is a deliberate paradox.

853.1.] Sacrapant's body must be removed, because Jack later (901.1) returns
with his head.

Jack. O sir, are you gone? Now I hope we shall have some
　　other coil. Now, master, how like you this? The   855
　　conjurer he is dead, and vows never to trouble us
　　more. Now get you to your fair lady, and see what you
　　can do with her.—Alas, he heareth me not all this
　　while, but I will help that.

He pulls the wool out of his ears.

Eumenides. How now, Jack! What news?   860
Jack. Here, master, take this sword and dig with it at the
　　foot of this hill.

He digs and spies a light.

Eumenides. How now, Jack! What is this?
Jack. Master, without this the conjurer could do nothing;
　　and so long as this light lasts, so long doth his art   865
　　endure; and this being out, then doth his art decay.
Eumenides. Why then, Jack, I will soon put out this light.
Jack. Ay, master, how?
Eumenides. Why, with a stone I'll break the glass, and then
　　blow it out.   870
Jack. No, master, you may as soon break the smith's anvil
　　as this little vial. Nor the biggest blast that ever
　　Boreas blew cannot blow out this little light—but she

S.D. 862.1. *He*] *Q.*; EUMENIDES *Dyce 1861*.   871. anvil] (anfill) *Q*.

---

854. *O sir, are you gone?*] Jack's reversal of the mood is similar to the actions of
the Vice in old plays:
　Ambidexter. [on seeing the wicked King Cambises dead]
　　How now noble king pluck up your hart:
　　What will you dye and from us depart?
　　Speake to me and ye be alive?
　　He cannot speake, but beholde how with death he doth strive.
　　Alas good King, alas he is gone:
　　The Devill take me, if for him I make any mone.
　　　　　　　　　　　　　　(Cambises, Tudor Facsimile Texts, F4)
　855. *coil*] rumpus. Again, like the Vice, Jack immediately thinks of a new
escapade.
　871. *anvil*] Q. 'anfill' preserves an earlier form of the word: 'anfeld' or
'anfelt'.
　873. *Boreas*] god of the north wind.

that is neither maid, wife, nor widow. Master, wind
this horn, and see what will happen.   875

He winds the horn.

Here enters VENELIA *and breaks the glass, and blows out
the light, and goeth in again.*

Jack. So, master, how like you this? This is she that ran
madding in the woods, his betrothed love that keeps
the cross. And now this light being out, all are
restored to their former liberty. And now, master, to
the lady that you have so long looked for.   880

He draweth a curtain, and there DELIA *sitteth asleep.*

Eumenides. God speed, fair maid sitting alone: there is
once.
God speed, fair maid: there is twice.
God speed, fair maid: that is thrice.
Delia. Not so, good sir, for you are by.
Jack. Enough, master. She hath spoke. Now I will leave   885
her with you.   [*Exit.*]
Eumenides. Thou fairest flower of these western parts,
    Whose beauty so reflecteth in my sight

881.] *as Q.; prose in Dyce.*   886. *Exit*] *Dyce.*

876–80.] In giving Jack these lines of synopsis, Peele is not awkwardly and
frantically trying to bring the multiple strands of action together. Jack acts as
master of ceremonies; his words give the audience a perspective on the whole.
The Vices do the same thing, and, in a more sophisticated way, so does
Prospero.

877. *his betrothed love*] i.e. the betrothed love of him.

880.1. draweth a curtain] compare *Tp.*, V.i.171.1, where Ferdinand and
Miranda are 'discovered' playing at chess.

881–3.] Eumenides' reaction to the revelation of the beloved object of his
quest is deliberately ritualised. He employs the formula for waking a sleeping
beauty. Richard Proudfoot suggested to me that 'sitting alone' is probably to be
repeated in lines 882 and 883. The repetition makes the meaning of Delia's
response (884) clearer.

884.] i.e. I am not sitting alone, for you are here. Delia's simple line of
recognition, at the instant of her awakening, following spontaneously upon
Eumenides' ritual lines, is one of the most startlingly beautiful moments in the
play.

As doth a crystal mirror in the sun—
For thy sweet sake I have crossed the frozen Rhine;   890
Leaving fair Po, I sailed up Danuby,
As far as Saba, whose enhancing streams
Cuts twixt the Tartars and the Russians.
These have I crossed for thee, fair Delia.
Then grant me that which I have sued for long.   895
Delia. Thou gentle knight, whose fortune is so good
    To find me out and set my brothers free,
    My faith, my heart, my hand I give to thee.
Eumenides. Thanks, gentle madam.—But here comes
    Jack. Thank him, for he is the best friend that we   900
    have.

Enter JACK *with a head in his hand.*

Eumenides. How now, Jack! What hast thou there?
Jack. Marry, master, the head of the conjurer.
Eumenides. Why, Jack, that is impossible. He was a young
    man.   905
Jack. Ah, master, so he deceived them that beheld him.
    But he was a miserable, old and crooked man, though
    to each man's eye he seemed young and fresh. For,

893. Cuts] *Q.;* Cut *Dyce.*

890–3.] perhaps based on Greene's *Orlando Furioso.* See Intro., p. 5.
Mandrecarde: I furrowd Neptunes Seas,
    Northeast as far as is the frosen Rhene,
    Leaving fair Voya, crost up Danuby,
    As hie as Saba whose inhauncing streames
    Cuts twixt the Tartares and the Russians:

                    (*Malone Society Reprints*, 72–6)
  892. *Saba*] Sheba. See Vulgate I Kings, x.1: '*Sed & regina Saba audita fama Solomonis.*' See also the note on the passage in *The Old Testament of the Jerusalem Bible*, New York, 1966. The Land of Saba may have been in Ethiopia or in Arabia (Yemen). Obviously, the journey described by Eumenides and Mandrecarde gives fanciful, rather than actual, geography. The intent of the passage is to convey a sense of a long quest, filled with marvels.
  893. *Cuts*] See 167n.
  908. *he seemed*] *he* and *see* are visible only in QH and QP. Portions of the *h* in *he* and the second *e* in *see* are visible in QB. In QD the page is missing and is supplied in facsimile from QB.

master, this conjurer took the shape of the old man
that kept the cross, and that old man was in the   910
likeness of the conjurer. But now, master, wind your
horn.

He winds his horn.

Enter VENELIA, *the* Two Brothers, *and* [ERESTUS,] *he that was at
the cross.*

Eumenides. Welcome, Erestus; welcome, fair Venelia;
    Welcome, Thelea and Calepha both!
    Now have I her that I so long have sought.   915
    So saith fair Delia, if we have your consent.
First Brother. Valiant Eumenides, thou well deservest
    To have our favours; so let us rejoice
    That by thy means we are at liberty.
    Here may we joy each in other's sight   920
    And this fair lady have her wandering knight.
Jack. So, master, now ye think you have done; but I must
    have a saying to you. You know you and I were
    partners: I to have half in all you got.
Eumenides. Why, so thou shalt, Jack.   925
Jack. Why, then, master, draw your sword. Part your
    lady. Let me have half of her presently.
Eumenides. Why, I hope, Jack, thou dost but jest! I prom-
    ised thee half I got, but not half my lady.
Jack. But what else, master? Have you not gotten her?   930

S.D. 912.1. *He*] *Q.;* EUMENIDES *Dyce 1861.*   S.D. 912.2. ERESTUS] *Dyce
1861.*   914. Calepha] (Kalepha) *Q.*   920. in other's] *Q. subst.;* in the
other's *conj. Dyce 1861.*

909–11. *this conjurer . . . conjurer*] The conjurer took Erestus' shape and gave
Erestus his own shape (an aged man).
    912.2 S.D. ERESTUS] transformed into a young man; see previous n.
    923. *saying to you*] something to say about that. See *Jew of Malta*, II.iii.90: 'I'll
have a saying to that nunnery.'
    926–46.] This episode, in which proof of friendship takes precedence over
love for the lady, is not meant to be played for psychological realism. Delia's
single line of acceptance (944) is the climax of a stylised scene.

Therefore divide her straight, for I will have half.
There is no remedy.

Eumenides. Well, ere I will falsify my word unto my
friend, take her all. Here, Jack, I'll give her thee.

Jack. Nay, neither more nor less, master, but even just   935
half.

Eumenides. Before I will falsify my faith unto my friend, I
will divide her. Jack, thou shalt have half.

First Brother. Be not so cruel unto our sister, gentle
knight!   940

Second Brother. O spare fair Delia! She deserves no death!

Eumenides. Content yourselves; my word is passed to him.
Therefore prepare thyself, Delia; for thou must die.

Delia. Then farewell world! Adieu, Eumenides!

He offers to strike and JACK *stays him.*

Jack. Stay, master! It is sufficient I have tried your con-   945
stancy. Do you now remember since you paid for the
burying of a poor fellow?

Eumenides. Ay, very well, Jack.

Jack. Then, master, thank that good deed for this good
turn. And so, God be with you all!   950

JACK *leaps down in the ground.*

Eumenides. Jack, what, art thou gone? Then, farewell,
Jack.—
Come, brothers, and my beauteous Delia,
Erestus, and thy dear Venelia.
We will to Thessaly with joyful hearts.

All. Agreed. We follow thee and Delia.   955

Exeunt omnes [except MADGE, FROLIC *and* FANTASTIC].

S.D. 944.1. *He*] Q.; EUMENIDES *Dyce 1861.*   951.] *as Dyce;* gone?/Then
Q.   S.D. 955.1. *except . . .* FANTASTIC] *Dyce 1861 subst.*

937–38. *I will divide her . . . half*] Though part of a prose speech, the sentence
is iambic pentameter, as is 942: 'Content yourselves; my word is passed to him.'
946. *since*] when.
951. Compare Jack's words at 854–5. Eumenides now takes over Jack's
function of supervisor of the action.

Fantastic. What, gammer, asleep?

Madge. By the mass, son, 'tis almost day; and my windows
shuts at the cock's crow.

Frolic. Do you hear, gammer? Methinks this Jack bore a
great sway amongst them.   960

Madge. O, man, this was the ghost of the poor man that
they kept such a coil to bury, and that makes him to
help the wandering knight so much. But, come, let us
in. We will have a cup of ale and a toast this morning—and so depart.   965

Fantastic. Then you have made an end of your tale, gammer?

Madge. Yes, faith. When this was done, I took a piece of
bread and cheese, and came my way. And so shall you
have too, before you go, to your breakfast. [*Exeunt.*] 970

FINIS

958. shuts] *Q.;* shut *Dyce 1861.*   964. toast] (tost) *Q.*   S.D. 970. *Exeunt*]
Dyce 1861.

957–8. *windows shuts*] See 167 n.

964. *toast*] For Q.'s spelling 'tost', see also Daniel's conjecture at 825.

965. *depart*] part.

968. *When this was done*] Note that Madge speaks in the past tense. From the
perspective of the present, the night's happenings have vanished 'as a tale that is
told'. Her words imply that she has done this many times before.

970. *to*] for.

Glossarial Index to the Commentary

This index lists words, phrases, names, tags, etc., which are elucidated in the Commentary. An asterisk before a word or a reference indicates that the meaning is not covered by *O.E.D.*